Long and Short Stitch Embroidery
A COLLECTION OF FLOWERS

Long and Short Stitch Embroidery

A Collection of Flowers

TRISH BURR

To Simon, with all my love.

First published in 2006 by
Sally Milner Publishing Pty Ltd
734 Woodville Road
BINDA   NSW   2583
AUSTRALIA

© Trish Burr 2006

Design: Anna Warren, Warren Ventures
Editing: Anne Savage
Photography: Tim Connolly Photography

Printed in China

National Library of Australia Cataloguing-in-Publication data:

Burr, Trish.
    Long and short stitch embroidery : a collection of flowers.

    ISBN-13 978 1 86351 352 4.

    ISBN-10 1 86351 352 3.

    1. Embroidery - Patterns. 2. Flowers in art. I. Title.
    (Series : Milner craft series).

    746.44041

Disclaimer
The information in this instruction book is presented in good faith. However, no warranty is given, nor
results guaranteed, nor is freedom from any patent to be inferred. Since we have no control over the
use of information contained in this book, the publisher and the author disclaim liability for untoward results.

10 9 8 7 6 5 4 3 2 1

Contents

Acknowledgements

GRATITUDE

In God I find a precious gift

That knows no fear, no feud

That glows so still, serene and pure

The gift of gratitude.

In seamless gratitude I weave

A silent healing prayer

With shining threads of ceaseless joy

For man is God's great heir.

VIOLET KER SEYMER

I have been fortunate enough to gain permission to use the following works for reproduction in embroidery and would like to express my gratitude to: Shirley Sherwood, author of *Passion for Flowers and Contemporary Botanical Art* (Cassell Publishing UK), for extracts used from the following botanical paintings: *Pansies* (Susannah Blaxill), *Hibiscus syriacus* (Jinyong Feng), *Iceland Poppies* (Katie Lee), *Glory Lily* (Pandora Sellars), *Magnolia* (Paul Jones) and *Hybrid Pansies* (Siriol Sherlock); and to Tracy Hall, UK, for watercolour paintings used in full or part, as follows: *Bearded Iris*, *Pink Poppies*, *Sweet Peas*. For further information on Tracy's gorgeous watercolour paintings on a variety of subjects, visit her website at www.hall75.freeserve.co.uk

All other flowers are reproduced from extracts of royalty-free calendars, prints, cards and books.

This book would not be complete without the encouragement and guidance of some wonderful members of the needlework world. I would like to thank Shelagh Amor, Tonie Evans, Audrey Francini, Tracy Franklin, Wendy James, Kay Stanis, Anna Scott and Julie Walsby for contributing tips and sharing so freely your knowledge and experience. It is encouraging to know that we are all working together for the universal good of the reader and student of embroidery. Two people in particular influenced this book and deserve a big thank you: Jeanmarie Brucia of Jenny June Fancy Work (see suppliers list) for suggesting areas that students found problematical in long and short stitch, which resulted in the groundwork for this book, and Canby Robertson, who guided and inspired and whose expertise is responsible for many of the tips that I am able to share. I would like to thank Sally Saunders at the Royal School of Needlework for her time and efforts in reviewing this book and the valued suggestions proffered under her guidance.

I can of mine own self do nothing ... the Father that dwelleth in me, He doeth the works

(JOHN 5:30, 14:10).

To Ian Webster and Penny Doust of Sally Milner Publishing, my thanks for encouraging me to pursue this title with renewed confidence. My editor Anne Savage and designer Anna Warren, who compile such professional craft publications for us and present them so beautifully—it is a pleasure to work with you.

This is always a good time to thank those nearest and dearest to me for their love and support: Mum and Dad, Boo and John, Mum Burr, Sue and Nigel, Pat, Gill and Janey. To my first class—Sheila, Jeannie, Joneta, Nola, Lucinda, Trish and Antoinette—I learnt so much from you all and will always be grateful for your enthusiasm and encouragement.

To Norma Young and my South African students for gently introducing me to the South African teaching world—I have enjoyed our lessons and your keen participation. These ladies have inspired a lot of the tips in this book—your split stitch tip is included, Norma!

To my husband Simon, who unstaples my stitching, washes the dishes, takes the kids to school and between bouts of golf patiently listens to my theories on the intricacies of embroidery! This has been a challenging year for us with our move to a new country, but you never let me give up believing this could become a reality. To my special girls Stacey, Tess and Katie—who are my life. Thanks to all of you for your love and support.

Preface

The most appropriate term for the style of embroidery I am demonstrating here would probably be 'threadpainting' or 'needlepainting' (my preference). The embroiderer can portray flowers in the same way as a botanical painter by using the appropriate stitch to create a three-dimensional form on a two-dimensional surface to realistically interpret their subject. The limitations of needle and thread mean that the work will look more like fine lines drawn with a pen rather than a brush, but the aim is to create an illusion of brushwork. It is virtually impossible to take something from nature and reproduce it on fabric with all its imperfections and details, for we have to compose an outline within which to work, and create an impression within this foundation.

There has been much discussion between the needlework guilds and organisations worldwide as to the many and varied terms used over the years for long and short stitch—silk shading, soft shading, long and short shading, and shaded satin stitch, to name a few. Each one is correct in its individual interpretation, dependent upon culture or era, but relies on the basic execution of long and short stitches which either overlap or interlock with each other to subtly blend shades of colour. Below are some examples of terms used for long and short stitch in different cultures which might explain the confusion that often arises between the different terminologies:

- Western—silk shading or soft shading (long and short stitches in the first row, thereafter long stitches only, split back into the previous rows).

- East Asia (Korea, China and Japan)—long and short stitch (long and short stitches in all rows, use of hidden stitch to bleed between previous rows).

- China—*shan tao* stitch (stitches worked in long and short between stitches, not split back into previous rows).

- Japanese—alternating long and short stitch, *nagamijika-sashinui* (long and short stitches in first row, thereafter long stitches worked in finer threads, split back into previous rows).

- Japanese—random long and short stitch, *midare-sashinui* (mixed-up long and short stitches, bleeding between stitches of previous rows, worked by area of colour).

Slight differences in the working of these methods sometimes result in slightly different effects, but to avoid confusion I will concentrate on the more common Western technique, here referred to as 'long and short stitch'.

As a trained embroiderer, I would like to congratulate Trish Burr for her courage and hard work in producing a book that provides a good introduction to this beautiful but challenging technique. I hope this book will play a part in encouraging readers to try Silk Shading.

Long and Short captivates all who see it worked, and my students over the past 50 years have always become very enthusiastic and keen to develop their skills by further study in this fascinating method of embroidery.

SALLY SAUNDERS

DIP. ROYAL SCHOOL OF NEEDLEWORK, ENGLAND

Introduction

I am a self-taught embroiderer who has gathered and acquired most of my knowledge through the use of books on the subject. At school I leaned towards the arts, but it was not until much later in life when I was married and had children that my interest in embroidery began to develop. At first it was cross-stitch (like most of us) which later expanded into surface embroidery.

Those of us who have grown up in Africa have long been used to finding the fabrics and threads required for embroidery in short supply or even non-existent. We became quite resourceful at finding alternatives such as sewing cotton or knitting wool to achieve the effect we needed. I was soon introduced to the joys of mail order and a credit card (much to the dismay of my husband!), which enabled me to gain access to the wonderful materials available on the wider market. My workroom (cupboard) is now a haven of books, threads, fabrics, hoops, needlework accessories and art supplies, and the computer is my constant companion. (As it is for most of us, it is more often a case of 'want' rather than 'need' when it comes to buying embroidery supplies!)

I love what I do with a passion and want to share this perfect antidote to the frenetic pace of modern life. My family patiently endures this need for self-expression, overlook the many loose threads attached to my trousers when I go out in public, share my highs and lows, and encourage my endless attempts to cram as much embroidery time into my day as possible! (Although once, when asked what she thought of my finished botanical embroidery, my three and a half year old said, 'It needs some grass at the bottom for the flower to grow into'!)

Over the years I have become fascinated with the shading aspects of surface and crewel embroidery and now tend to favour botanical subjects. There is no greater joy than to re-create these floral beauties in thread, a joy which culminated in my first book, *Redouté's Finest Flowers in Embroidery*. Since then I have had opportunities to commune with seasoned needleworkers from all over the world, who have been kind enough to pass on their pearls of wisdom. Their generosity motivated me to offer classes on the subject. As a result of this hands-on experience I have seen the embroidery process anew, through the eyes of the learner, which has led me to include a few more vital ingredients into my 'good recipe'. You will find in this book a whole new section on long and short stitch, plus tips for colour blending.

Most of us would consider a good recipe to have step-by-step instructions and lots of pictures to guide us—which I have tried to provide—but this book is not a paint-by-numbers affair! Each design will be interpreted differently by each individual embroiderer. You should never try to mimic the style of your neighbour. Embroidery is an art form and as such must express your innate individuality. Take what you learn from this book and develop your own approach to this style of embroidery. The great American artist Georgia O'Keeffe once said, 'I don't see why we ever think of what others think of what we do—no matter who they are. Isn't it enough just to express yourself?'

For those of you who have never attempted this type of embroidery before, take heart—you do not have to be a botanical artist to achieve this effect and it is not as hard as it looks. With a bit of practise you will soon be up, running and addicted! It is a good idea to have a 'doodle cloth' (practice fabric) handy, mounted in a hoop, to try out the techniques before putting them into use in any of the projects. Begin with the starter projects to familiarise yourself with the technique and read over the tips for working the designs. Remember that preparation is all important to the result of your work—you cannot afford to skip the groundwork. If you are having problems in a specific area refer to the list of tips and you should find the answer.

This time I have included works from the Shirley Sherwood Collection and Tracy Hall's flower paintings, which have been a great privilege to reproduce, as they lend themselves so perfectly to this style of embroidery. I have tried to gently introduce the novice, but at the same time challenge the expert, by providing a range of projects from simple to challenging. I have thoroughly enjoyed compiling this book, and it is my great hope that it will be a beneficial and enjoyable learning experience for each one of you.

Materials

Fabric

Any kind of medium weight cotton or linen fabric can be used for this type of embroidery, as long as it does not stretch. The general requirement is that it should be closely woven and of medium weight.

Any kind of embroidery taking up a large proportion of the fabric needs to be kept taut in a hoop or frame. If the fabric is stretched while the embroidery is in progress it will contract and become distorted when removed from the hoop.

Suitable cotton fabrics include:

- calico
- any type of medium weight closely-woven cotton
- cotton satin.

Suitable linen fabrics include:

- very fine Italian linen union
- church linen
- any type of medium weight closely-woven linen
- dowlas.

Backing fabric

Backing fabric is used to support the main fabric if it is lightweight. (Ensure that you line up the grains of both fabrics very carefully to prevent puckering.)

Suitable backing fabrics include:

- muslin (first choice)
- lightweight cotton
- lightweight calico.

Threads

I have mainly used DMC Mouliné special 6-strand cotton, which is available in approx 480 colours. DMC 6-strand embroidery floss is the most widely sold embroidery thread in the world and to my mind is the best quality. It is composed of six easily separated strands, so that you can use one or more strands of the same colour, or mix colours to obtain a shaded effect. It is made from the finest long staple cottons, and is the result of years of experience. Double mercerisation gives the cottons a high sheen and they are absolutely colourfast and fade-resistant, ensuring your work can be passed from generation to generation.

A few years ago I had the good fortune to visit the DMC factory in Mulhouse, France, where we saw the thread production. It is a humbling experience to see the intensive process involved in producing the finished skein of thread. To reproduce consistent dye lots, strict adherence to previous dye solutions is monitored under the carefully critical eye of colour checkers who have spent many years perfecting the art and are employed solely for this task. Despite this, it remains important to purchase enough thread from the same dye lot to complete the one embroidery, as dye lots unavoidably differ, even if only to the slightest degree.

When I am unable to find a particular shade in the DMC range I have substituted with colours from Coats & Crafts Anchor stranded cotton, which again has an extensive range of good quality thread, suitable for this type of work. Use threads from either range in an effort to find just the right shade.

OTHER THREADS

These projects could also be stitched using silk or crewel wool, as long as the colour range is sufficient to provide the colours required. Because crewel wool is thicker than cotton you will have to adjust your filling slightly or alternatively enlarge the design to accommodate it. Crewel wool can be successfully used in conjunction with cotton or silk but ensure that you work the cotton or silk first as they will combine better. If using crewel wool you will have to use a heavyweight fabric such as linen twill to support the weight of the wool.

Crewel wool is particularly suitable for learning to stitch in long and short stitch as the hairiness of the wool is very forgiving. Appleton's Crewel wool is my recommendation, as it has a good range of colours and is colourfast.

Shade card

Get yourself a shade card for the brand of thread you are using; it will prove an invaluable tool when choosing colours. Try to use a brand that has a good colour selection as you can never have enough colours for this style of embroidery.

HOOPS AND FRAMES

An embroidery hoop or frame is essential for this type of embroidery as it is imperative that the fabric be kept very taut as you work, to prevent distortion.

Hoops

A wooden hoop, known as a tambour or ring, is made up of two hoops, one inside the other, the outer hoop with a screw for tightening the fabric. It is best to use a deep-sided hoop, similar to the kind used

Thread tips

- Pull out the number of strands you wish to use in the one action, not as single strands.

- Keep your thread length at a maximum of about 50 cm (20 in), to prevent tangling and knotting.

- If you do get a knot, pull the loop of the knot towards you and this will usually release it.

- Dangle your needle and thread from the back of your work at intervals to undo twists and prevent tangling.

for quilting. Hoops are available in different sizes; use the smallest hoop that you can without encroaching too much on the design. The border between the design and the hoop edge should be a minimum of 2 cm (¾ in).

To avoid the risk of the hoop leaving a dirty ring on your work it is recommended that you bind all hoops before putting the embroidery fabric in place. To do this take bias binding (opened out flat) or a narrow strip of waste cotton fabric and bind it around the inner hoop, catching the end with a couple of stitches to prevent slipping. Alternatively, you can place a piece of white tissue paper over the area before replacing the outer ring, then tear away the tissue paper from the working area, leaving a ring around the edge.

Place the fabric (and backing) over the inner hoop, place the outer hoop on top and push over. Tighten the fabric as much as possible and then adjust the screw until drum tight.

It is not advisable to use a hoop when stitching with silk thread unless it is washable, as it may be difficult to remove the ring marks. Use a frame instead. Remove the hoop at the end of each stitching session to prevent ring marks, which may be difficult to remove, developing on any fabric.

When you have tightened the fabric in the hoop as much as possible, hold it over the steam from a kettle until just damp. Allow to dry and the fabric will become drum tight.

Frames

My new preference is for an artist's four-sided canvas stretcher frame. These can be bought unassembled in various sizes at any good art shop; this enables you to make up the specific size you need.

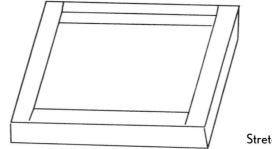

Stretcher frame

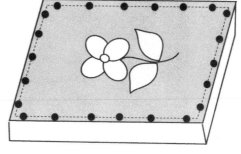

Fabric stretched and tacked onto frame

Centre the fabric over the front of the frame and secure on the back with drawing pins, tacks or a staple gun, easing the fabric into place so that it is taut over the frame. There are various types of frames on the market and the choice is dependent upon trial and error and what suits you best. Frames have the added advantage over hoops of keeping your fabric taut without developing weakened areas caused by screw openings, and they do not leave ring marks. When you have completed the stitching you can leave the work on the frame, wash it in mild soapy water and leave till dry—your work will lie beautifully flat without any distortion or puckering.

Tips for working with a hoop or frame

- When you have tightened the fabric in the hoop as much as possible, hold it over the steam from a kettle or a saucepan of boiling water until just damp. Allow to dry and the fabric will become drum tight. Use the flick test to ensure that the fabric is drum tight (flick the fabric and it should make a 'ping' sound).

- Make sure that you line up the grain of the fabric with the frame so that you will be working with the grain and not against it; misalignment is the main cause of distortion. (See preparing the fabric, page 18.)

SCISSORS

You will need a small, sharp pair of embroidery scissors for cutting threads. It is worth spending a little extra and getting the best pair that you can afford. Be brutal in your resolution to keep your embroidery scissors for cutting threads only—not fabric, paper or anything else. This is a constant bone of contention in my house—even now, after years of threatening dire retribution, I far too often find my precious scissors blunt and covered with glue, having been misappropriated for use on thick cardboard homework projects!

NEEDLES

There are quite a number of different needles suitable for various needlecraft projects. The choice can be confusing so I will keep to the basics needed for the embroidery designs in this book. Always buy the best quality needles you can afford. As soon as the needle you are using becomes blackened or does not slip easily through the fabric, change it for a new one.

Recommended needles

Crewel embroidery needles (for most embroidery stitches):

- size 10 for one strand of thread
- size 9 for two strands of thread
- size 8 for three or more strands

Straw or milliner's needles (for French knots or bullion knots):

- size 4 for one/two strands of thread
- size 3 for two/three strands of thread

My favourite brands are Milwards and
DMC, but your preference may be for
other brands.

PENCILS

Water-soluble pens are not suitable for
fine work as the lines are too thick, but
they could be used for crewel work. Be
very careful when using water-soluble
pens, for although the colour appears to
have washed out, the lines can reappear
when dry.

When using a pencil to draw on to your
fabric it is advisable to use a fairly hard
lead pencil. A Berol Verifine lead pencil in
white can be used for dark fabrics. If the
fabric you are using is textured it may be
difficult to obtain a smooth line with a
hard pencil, in which case you can use a
softer one such as an HB. These pencils
are available at any good art shop.

Techniques

PREPARING THE FABRIC

It is best to wash your fabric first in hot water to pre-shrink it and remove any dirty marks, then iron with a steam iron. Always choose the best quality you can afford and cut a generous size to allow for mounting or making up, leave an allowance of at least 10 cm (4 in) around the design.

Grain of the fabric

Find the grain of the fabric by pulling out a thread on two sides at right angles to each other, so that the grain is lined up before mounting and stitching. Ensure that these grains line up with the right angle of your frame when mounting. This will prevent distortion of work when completed.

TRANSFERRING A DESIGN

Outlines for transferring the designs are supplied; they can be used actual size, or reduced or enlarged according to your personal preference. The easiest way to do this is by photocopying. Do remember that if you reduce a design in size, the number of embroidery stitches will also be reduced, and could limit the shading that can be applied, just as enlarging a design will increase the number of stitches needed to fill the outlines. You cannot reduce or enlarge the actual stitch sizes, as this will give a very uneven finish. Remember to increase the size of the background fabric if you choose to enlarge a design.

There are a number of ways to transfer a design onto fabric, but by far the easiest is to place the fabric on top of the design, with a light source behind the design, and trace over the design with an HB pencil.

Tracing methods

*   Use a light box.
*   Place a light under a glass table.
*   Hold fabric and design up against a glass window (you will need to attach both with masking tape to prevent movement).

Another method uses fabric carbon paper; in this case you place the carbon between the design and the fabric (design on top, fabric underneath) and draw over the design with a sharp pencil. Graphite carbon paper is the best type to use, but check at intervals to see that the lines are being transferred.

Directional lines

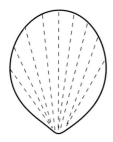

Vertical guidelines

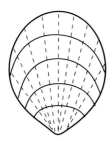

Horizontal guidelines added

It is helpful to draw directional lines (guidelines) onto the fabric after transferring the design. These will help guide your stitches towards the base of the shape. Place the first guideline down the centre and work others on either side of this. You can put in as many guidelines as you like. The lines should radiate from the centre point of the shape outwards. You may wish to draw in horizontal guidelines as well, following the contours of the shape, to guide your rows of shading, but be careful that your rows do not become too regimented, causing hard lines of colour. You will have to encroach some of the lines to give a staggered effect. Decide on the number of shades you are going to use on the motif and divide the motif equally to accommodate them.

Starting and ending off

There are many ways to secure your thread at the start of your work. After much trial and error I have found the method outlined here to be the most suitable, as it does not leave any lumps and bumps.

Starting off

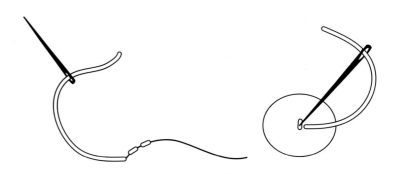

Make a few small running stitches in an area to be covered by embroidery or directly on the design line. Start about 10 mm (⅓ in) away from the point you wish to start and work the running stitches back towards this point. Leave a short tail of about 12 mm (½ in). Start stitching and these running stitches will be covered as you work.

Ending off

When ending off, work a few running stitches in a place to be covered as before, and cut off close to the fabric.

If you have run out of working space (in other words, the motif is completed) you can work your thread into the back of the work with a few small stitches. Try to catch some of the fabric while doing this to make sure it is very secure.

NB It is best not to carry your thread across long stretches at the back of the work. Rather, end off and start again.

COMPLETION OF WORK

Washing and pressing

If the work is clean, lightly spray it with water, place face down on a fluffy towel and press it on the back (this will not flatten the design). Do not slide the iron across the back of the work. If it is necessary to wash your work, double-check that you have used washable and colourfast threads and that your fabric is pre-shrunk. Work that does not meet these conditions cannot be washed as the fabric will shrink, causing massive puckering of the stitching and the thread colours will run—throw it in the dustbin and start again! Wash in tepid (lukewarm) water with a mild soap, rinse, and roll up in a fluffy towel. While still damp, place the work face down on the towel and press until dry.

If a design has been worked in crewel wool, it should be blocked rather than pressed (see below).

Blocking

If the work has become distorted or the fabric puckered, it may be necessary to block it, to stretch it back into shape. There are two ways of doing this.

Wash the work first (if necessary) and dry it. Take a square frame (or an upholstered frame) of suitable size and place the work on top of it, using small tacks or pins to fix two opposite sides to the frame. (A square frame is an artist's stretcher frame similar to the type used to frame a picture; an upholstered frame is covered in foam, then fabric. The fabric is stretched over a square frame and stapled directly into the wood, but on an upholstered frame the fabric is stretched across and pinned into the foam cover.) Stretch the fabric across until it is squarely on the frame and tack or pin the other two sides. Alternatively, you can use a piece of hardboard covered with dressmaker's graph paper. Line the fabric up squarely using the graph paper as a guide, and tack your work to the hardboard.

When the work is squarely and securely tacked in place, dampen the fabric with water in a mist sprayer, or hold the back of the fabric over a steaming kettle until damp. Leave it until it is completely dry (a couple of hours, or as long as necessary) and remove the tacks. The fabric will spring back into shape and the stitching will be smooth and even.

Mounting

If you would like to frame your work you can either take it to a professional framer who will stretch and mount it for you, or mount it and frame it yourself. This can be done using one of the self-adhesive mounting boards that are available especially for the purpose, or you can tape the work onto a piece of board with masking tape.

I asked my local framer how he mounted needlework and this is what he said: The fabric is dampened and then stretched onto a piece of mount board. It is then stapled around the edges with a staple gun or taped down with masking tape (depending on the weight of the fabric) and left to dry. This is the only method that ensures that there are no creases or puckers in the fabric.

1 Position the mount board centrally on the back of your design. Fold one edge of the fabric over and push pins through the fabric and board along one edge.

2 Stretching the fabric gently, pull it across to the opposite side, fold edge over and pin.

3 Starting from one end, lace the fabric as shown from one side to the other, crossing the threads.

4 Now pin and lace the other two sides in the same manner. Fold in and slipstitch the corners. Once all four sides are laced, remove the pins. Your work should be taut and even.

Using the finished embroidery

There are several ways to make up finished work: as a framed picture, cushion cover, book cover, greeting card, pincushion, bag (handbag, toilet bag, lingerie bag, utility bag), as a centrepiece for a quilt or bedspread, or as table mats. You can also use it on one of the pre-finished accessories available on the market. I recently saw an embroidery incorporated into a canvas cushion. It had been stitched to the centre of the canvas cushion, with various freestyle canvas stitches and patterns stitched up to and covering the edge of the embroidery—it really was very effective! There are no rules today and a little imagination can go a long way.

Tips for working the designs

❏ Prepare your fabric, line up the grain and wash and iron before use.

❏ Trace the outline onto the fabric, following the transfer instructions.

❏ Fill in details and direction lines with a pencil, following the padding and details illustrations for the project you are working.

❏ Tack the backing fabric (if any) in place.

❏ Mount the fabric into a hoop or frame following the instructions. Use the flick test to ensure it is drum tight.

❏ Use the embroidery key as a guide to thread colours, and the colour photo for details on shading.

❏ Follow the step-by-step embroidery directions for the particular project.

❏ Each motif contributes to the final appearance so concentrate on individual images rather than trying to create the whole picture. As you complete each motif the final picture will start to unfold and come together.

❏ Always work from the background towards the foreground.

❏ Work a split/stem stitch outline around the shapes first to raise one shape against another. Complete the filling for each shape in sequence before stitching an outline around the next shape.

❏ Work stems in stem stitch or split stitch.

❏ Work the padded areas, if any.

- ❏ Leave a gap between pieces of padding to create a three-dimensional illusion.

- ❏ When using long and short stitch, always work from the outside in unless the directions say otherwise.

- ❏ Work centre leaf veins in split stitch in the lightest shade used in the leaf or stem unless the directions say otherwise.

- ❏ If you are uncertain about the way a flower is constructed, study a living flower if possible, and work accordingly.

- ❏ Stems always come from the midpoint of the leaf end, and from the centre of the flower.

- ❏ Do not try to put in every little plant detail in the first layer of stitching; rather, work these in afterwards.

- ❏ A flower has a centre; the petals have to be attached to this centre, which contain stamens or lumps of pollen. The petals should be worked towards this centre and any stamens or pollen added afterwards. If this is not always obvious, take apart a real flower to understand better how it works.

- ❏ If you find it difficult to incorporate areas of light and dark within a motif you can add these in afterwards (on top of the basic shading). These can be worked in staggered satin stitches (straight stitches) or free long and short stitches.

- ❏ Take time off from your work and stand back occasionally. Put your piece in a place where you pass by often and view it from afar—the effect will be quite different and encouraging.

Stitch glossary

BULLION KNOT

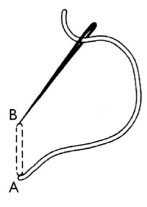

STEP 1 Using 2 strands of thread and needle size 10 bring the needle up at A and down at B.

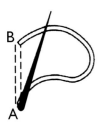

STEP 2 Bring the needle partly up at A, leaving a long loop.

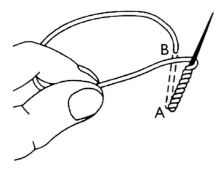

STEP 3 Hold the loop between thumb and forefinger and wind thread around the needle anti-clockwise. The number of loops depends upon the length of the bullion required. Ten loops will give you a long bullion, 20 loops a very long one.

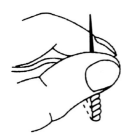

STEP 4 Hold the needle and coil with the thumb and forefinger of one hand and pull the needle gently through the coil with the other hand.

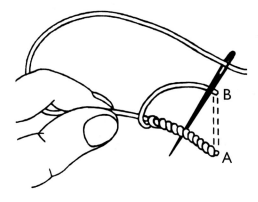

STEP 5 Push the top of the coil down while pulling the thread through. Even out the coil by pushing it along the thread until it lies flat on the fabric.

STEP 6 Re-insert the needle at B and take the thread through ready to start the next stitch.

FRENCH KNOT

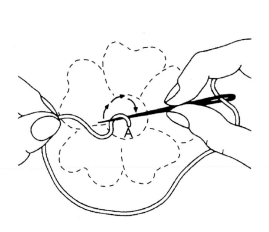

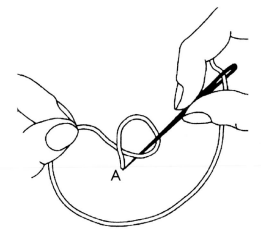

STEP 1 Using 2 strands of thread and straw needle size 4, bring the thread up at A. Hold the thread between thumb and forefinger as illustrated. Loop the thread over the needle once.

STEP 2 Insert the needle into the fabric at A, close to the original hole but not in the same hole.

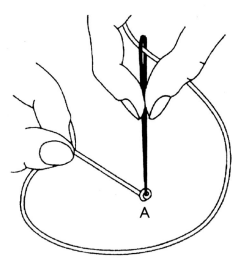

STEP 3 Pull the loop taut to form the knot.

LONG AND SHORT STITCH

Long and short stitch is also referred to as silk shading, soft shading, long and short shading or needlepainting, as the varying stitch lengths which encroach on each other lend this technique wonderfully to shading and give a realistic 'painted' finish. Long and short stitch is used as a filling stitch for all types of larger shapes, and is the most widely used stitch in this book and therefore worth spending time practising. There are a few ground rules for long and short stitch that we will explore in the techniques which follow; once you have mastered these we can look at ideas for enhancing the stitch by various means.

BASIC LONG AND SHORT STITCH

This is the basis of long and short stitch, worked in one direction only. It is quite often referred to as tapestry shading and can be used to fill in areas such as backgrounds. It is a good way to learn the stitch before embarking on the directional method.

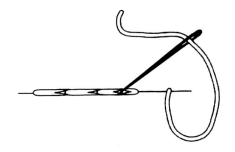

STEP 1 Outline the edges of the shape with split stitch. (You can use stem stitch for a more raised outline.) Use 1 strand of the lightest shade of thread required for that element of the design to work the outline. (I have used a darker thread in the photograph for the purpose of demonstration.) The split stitch forms the foundation for the long and short stitch infill.

not make your stitches too small, as this will give an uneven finish. The long stitches should be approximately 12 mm (½ in) in length and the short stitches about three-quarters of that length, 9 mm (⅜ in).

Work the 2nd row in long stitch only, using the next darkest shade of thread. In this row bring the needle up through the fabric to split the ends of the previous stitches, and down into the fabric. Although these stitches are worked in long stitch only, vary their lengths slightly to give a soft uneven line, not a straight one. Long and short stitch is intended to produce soft blending tones so avoid abrupt changes of tone.

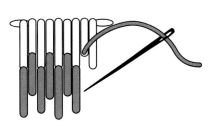

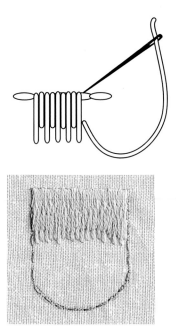

STEP 2 Work the first row in long and short stitch, using the lightest shade of thread. Bring the needle up inside the shape and down over the split stitch edge, as this will ensure a neat even edge. Do

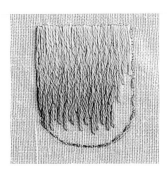

STEP 3 Work the 3rd and subsequent rows as for the 2nd row. Continue to change the shades of thread to create a shaded look.

DIRECTIONAL LONG AND SHORT STITCH

Filling a shape such as a petal

Shading does not always follow a straight course but can take different directions. If you study the structure of a petal, for example, you will see that it most often tapers towards the centre. The direction of stitches is most important and we need to know how to direct our stitches to follow the shape of a motif.

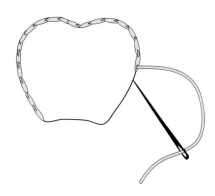

Long and short stitch is worked in five basic steps outlined below:

- Outline the motif to be stitched

- Draw directional guidelines into the shape.

- Work the foundation (first) row of long and short stitches

- Work the second row in staggered long stitches

- Complete the motif.

STEP 2 Pencil in the guidelines following the guideline instructions on page 19, drawing in the guideline down the centre of the motif, then splitting the halves in half again as shown. You can draw in as many lines as you need.

STEP 1 Choose approximately 4 shades of yarn from light to dark. Outline the shape with split/stem stitch with the lightest shade of yarn. Stem stitch will give a more padded raised edge. This edge will form the foundation for the shape to be worked.

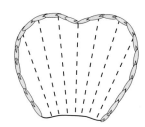

STEP 3 Work the first row in long and short stitch, using the lightest shade of thread. Start from the centre tip of the petal and work towards one side as shown. Come up in the shape and down

over the split stitch edge—this allows you to control the stitches, resulting in a precise, neat border.

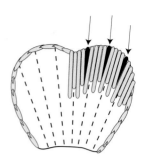

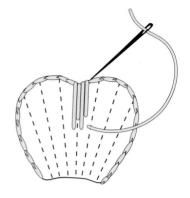

Shorten the stitch lengths when you reach the side to fit the curve. The stitches should be closely packed together with only a fibre between them so that the fabric is well covered, but not on top of each other so that they are overcrowded. This row forms the foundation for the successive rows, and needs to provide sufficient cover to work these rows into.

Remember to keep your stitches a good length, approximately 10 mm (⅜ in) for long stitches and 7 mm (¼ in) for short stitches (when working in wool, lengthen these slightly). If the stitches become too short the work will not look smooth.

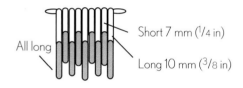

All long
Short 7 mm (¼ in)
Long 10 mm (³/8 in)

Complete the row by working from the centre tip towards the other side.

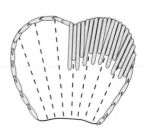

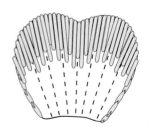

Add an extra small wedge stitch occasionally to adjust for the tapering shape (see wedge stitch instructions, page 34). This stitch will subtly alter the direction of subsequent stitches.

STEP 4 Work the 2nd row in *long stitch only*, using the next darkest shade of thread. Again work from the centre out towards one side and then the other. (You may find it easier to turn your work around so that you are working into the shape.) Work every third or fourth stitch and then go back and fill in the gaps, keeping in line with the direction lines and reducing the amount of stitches if the shape narrows.

Split *up* through the ends of the stitches of the previous row (about one-third of the way back) and *down* into the motif. If necessary, split further back into some stitches to stagger them (see instructions, page 36). Angle your needle close to the fabric when splitting up through the stitches to prevent holes forming.

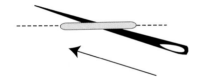

Complete the row as shown here.

Follow the guidelines as closely as possible and work long stitches only, staggering each stitch and varying their lengths so that the row of stitching does not form a straight line.

STEP 5 Subsequent rows—after the first row of long and short stitches is established, each succeeding row should be worked as for row two, and the stitches should be a similar length, but not regimented. No two stitches of the same length should lie next to each other, they should be staggered, creating an irregular line, so that the rows merge and encroach into each other.

Continue working each row, changing to the next shade of colour each time and reducing the number of stitches to fit the shape where necessary, until you reach the base of the motif. When you get to the last row the stitches will revert back to long and short.

Hold your work away from you and check there are no definite lines between shades. If there are, go back and add in a few long stitches here and there, tucking them in between existing stitches, to break up the line.

TIPS FOR IMPROVING YOUR
LONG AND SHORT STITCH

It is not necessary to memorise each and every one of these tips to ensure successful blending! This section is simply a troubleshooter for you to refer to in case of difficulties in an area.

General

- **Stitching method** Always stab stitch, never scoop.

Stab stitching.
Needle inserted straight through the fabric. Note the fabric remains taut.

Scoop stitching.
Needle inserted in and out in one movement. Note the fabric gives way to allow needle to pass through.

- **Tension** Keep the fabric drum tight in a hoop or frame—this helps to keep a good tension on the yarn. Keep a good stitch tension, not so tight so that the fabric puckers, but not so loose that the stitches float above the fabric. The reason one person's work will look smoother than another's is due to tension.

- **Raised outlines** Outline each motif on a design with split or stem stitch to ensure a neat, padded edge. These edges define areas within a design/motif.

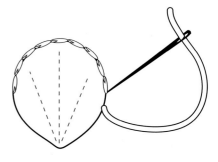

- **Colours** The correct choice of colours, values and tones is all important in good blending (see colour blending, page 38).

First row

- **Where to start** Start the first row in the centre of the outside edge. Wherever possible direct your stitches from the wider section down towards the narrow section of a motif. It is much easier to decrease the number of stitches than it is to increase the number.

- **Work over the split stitch edge**
  On the first row take the stitches from inside the shape and over the split stitch edge—-your needle should push firmly against the split stitch edge and angle slightly under it towards the back. This will result in a neat, precise edge.

- **Keep the stitches close together**
  Work the stitches close together to form a good foundation for placement of stitches in subsequent rows. The stitches should lie very close together, leaving no fabric showing, but not on top of each other.

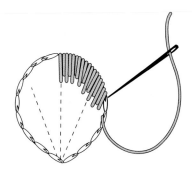

- **Draw in extra guidelines** You may find it helpful to draw in extra guidelines and stitch every long stitch in line with these guidelines first, before going back and filling in the short, long and wedge stitches in between as shown.

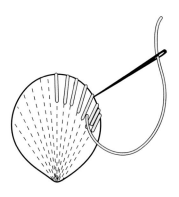

- **Keep in line with the guidelines**
  Keep in line with your guidelines at all times to ensure correct direction of stitches. To do this, try to line up the long stitches with the guidelines as much as possible and use the short stitches to change direction if needed.

- **Avoid abrupt changes of angle** The stitches in the first row should lie adjacent to each other; if one stitch changes path it will spoil the flow of the work. Avoid abrupt changes of angle in your stitching.

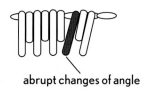

abrupt changes of angle

- **Use wedge stitches to change direction** When you need to change direction or are working around a curve, use wedge stitches to subtly alter the direction of your stitches. A wedge stitch is an extra short stitch placed between a long and short stitch.

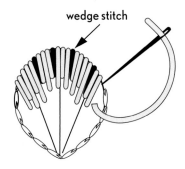

wedge stitch

- **How to insert a wedge stitch**

a   Tuck the base of the extra short stitch in next to the long stitch, then work the next short stitch slightly in front of the wedge so that it covers the base. The inside ends of these two stitches (short and wedge) will merge as one stitch at the base but will occupy the space of two stitches at the top. This gradually moves your long and short stitches around the shape of a curve.

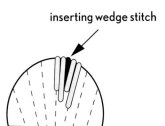

inserting wedge stitch

b   Never place two wedge stitches next to each other, but work them gradually around the curve.

c   All wedge stitches should be short stitches.

d   Wedge stitches can only be worked in the first row where they cannot be seen.

- **Shorten stitches to fit the side of a curve** When you reach the side of a shape you need to adjust the stitch lengths to fit the curve (shorten them slightly).

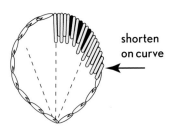

shorten on curve

- **Working the sides of a shape** Depending on the shape, either work the stitches toward the edge of the shape, or down the side of the shape. When working *straight down* a side these stitches will be almost parallel to the sides and tucked just inside the edge.

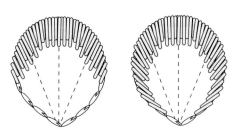

- **Pull aside the thread on side stitches** If you have difficulty placing the side stitches, you may find it helpful to pull aside the previous stitch with your finger as shown.

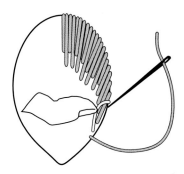

- **Follow the curve of a shape** The rows should follow the curve of the shape—do not work them in straight lines, as this will result in bands of colour.

correctly curved rows

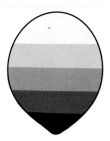

avoid straight bands of colour

- **To achieve smooth blending around a curve** When stitching a curved motif shorten your stitches somewhat

and increase the number of values. The extra value changes will make for a smoother transition of colour and the curve will appear more even.

Subsequent rows

- **Where to start** Again, start in the centre and work out towards either side.

- **Work into the shape** It is helpful to turn your work around and work into the shape so that you can see where you are going, but do whatever you feel comfortable with.

- **Work long stitches only** In the second row work long stitches only. The first row provides the staggered foundation for all the subsequent rows, so there is no need to work both long and short stitches in the following rows.

- **Vary the lengths of the long stitches** Do not rigidly follow the long and short pattern of the first row—work long stitches only but vary their lengths; never start or finish in the same place to avoid hard lines and give a soft look to your shading. Hold your work away from you and check to see that the rows are gently blending into each other without any rigid lines of colour. Long and short stitch ought to produce gentle lines and blending tones, not hard lines or abrupt changes, so the adjacent stitches should never finish at the same level. If necessary go back and add a stitch to break up a hard line.

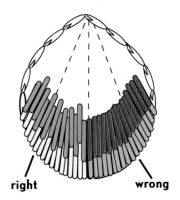

right   wrong

- **Avoid overcrowding of stitches**
  Be careful not to overfill an area. As the shape tapers down you will need to use less stitches to cover the fabric. Work every third or fourth short stitch first, then go back and fill in the gaps as needed to prevent overcrowding. If the shape narrows considerably you may have to skip a few more stitches and come back and fill in the space with the number of stitches needed to cover the fabric. You can work two long stitches into the same point at intervals to adjust for the narrowing space. These merged stitches can be treated as one stitch in subsequent rows.

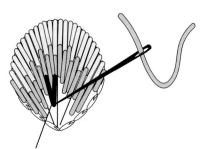

Merging stitches to be treated as one by working two long stitches into the same point

- **Split right back into previous stitches** Split about one-third of the way back into the previous stitches, or further if you are short of space.

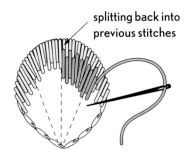

splitting back into previous stitches

- **Tips for splitting stitches**
a Ensure that you always split the yarn of the previous row, as this anchors down the previous stitches, preventing floating stitches that stand out and spoil the flow of your work.

b Always split up *through* stitches from the previous row (not between stitches), otherwise you will end up with 'pepper marks' (holes) that are impossible to get rid of. Splitting the yarn anchors down the stitches and prevents floating stitches (stitches that lie above the surface) that catch the eye and make the work look untidy.

c You do not need to split every stitch— as the shape tapers down you will need to compensate by reducing the amount of stitches to prevent overcrowding. Decide where you think a stitch needs to go and split into the nearest stitch of the previous row. Each new row anchors down the row before it.

d   Always split stitches with your needle by coming up through the stitches from the underside of your work so that the individual fibres on the stitch are pulled up. Never split by going down.

- **Angle your needle**   When splitting up through the stitches you need to bring your needle up at a low angle from underneath, close to your fabric (as shown), rather than coming straight up through the stitch. This will prevent holes forming and give a nice smooth look to your blending. If working into your shape (towards the base) your needle will be angled away from you.

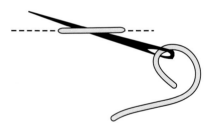

- **Deciding where the next stitch will go**   To decide where the next stitch will go in an unworked area, use the tip of your needle to trace the line of the stitch to the intended entry point before taking your thread down. Keep in line with your directional lines at all times. If the direction lines are strongly curved, keep angling the next stitch away from the previous one, towards the guideline, until you are lined up again.

- **Keep your shading smooth**   To ensure smooth shading keep your stitches a good length, for if they become too small your work will look rough and bumpy. Do not shorten them because you are worried that you will run out of space—you can always split further back into the previous row if necessary to fit in all your colours. If your shades of colour are fairly close you could stitch alternate shades in the second or subsequent row as follows:

Colour No 1 = first row long and short stitches

Colour No 2 = lengthen all the short stitches in the first row

Colour No 3 = lengthen all the long stitches in the first row.

- **Smoothing your stitches**   To smooth out your blended stitches comb the surface, over the split entry spots, with the point of your needle. The holes will disappear.

- **What good shading should look like** Your shading should look smooth and well blended. When the rows meet they should encroach into each other, not meet at a hard line. If you hold your work away from yourself and look at it through half-closed eyes the shades should appear to run into each other.

COLOUR BLENDING IN LONG AND SHORT STITCH

Good blending in long and short stitch is dependent upon the correct choice of colour and values, therefore it is helpful to understand a bit about colour theory when using it in a design. Colour is described in three dimensions—hue, value and intensity:

Hue The name of the colour, for example, blue or green-blue.

Value The degree of lightness or darkness of a colour, for example, light blue, medium blue or dark blue.

Intensity The degree of brightness or dullness of a colour, for example, bright blue or dull blue.

- Use as many values as you can to ensure a smooth blending of colour. Below are examples of shading from light to dark in a variety of common colours.

- It is important to provide a good contrast of values, from very light to very dark, otherwise your design will look flat and uninteresting.

- When choosing colours use a shade card and make sure you are in a good light (preferably daylight)

- If you are not sure which hue to pick from your colour chart, choose the duller intensity rather than the brighter one, as this will look more realistic and not dominate the design

- You will see that your shade card is made up of colour families. Combine hues from families that are similar, as this creates more interest than values that are all from the one family. For example, take pale and light orange and blend with medium and dark orange-red, making sure that the intensities of light orange and medium orange-red are similar so that there is not a drastic change of hue and intensity in one leap, otherwise it will jump out at you. Below are some examples of using values from different families together:

- If you have to change dramatically from one colour to another, exaggerate the staggering of the stitches to ensure a smooth blending. Here is an example of sudden colour changes:

- When the motif curves, add more colour values. This shortens the length of the stitches, making the curve more even. (Just as you do with stem or split stitch when working around the curve—you shorten them.)

- It is always best to shade from the wider section of the motif down towards the narrower section, so sometimes you will need to shade from dark to light, and the lighter colours will appear to be sitting on top of the darker colours. To correct this illusion, shorten the length of the lightest value and add another row of shading with a lighter value OR add another row of shading with the same light value as the previous row. This pins down any floating stitches. Here is an example of shading from dark to light:

- Sometimes it is necessary to change shades across a row—changing values mid-line can also help to break up a straight line of shading and prevent horizontal bands of colour appearing.

- Sometimes you will need to scatter the colours randomly within a motif to achieve a realistic effect. I have detailed this in the needlepainting section below, under scattering colours.

- If you are unable to find the right shade/hue on your colour chart, try mixing two colours to create it. To do this you need to stitch both colours (one strand of each) alternately, thus creating the illusion of the right colour (if using 2 strands of thread you can mix them in the needle).

- Remember that smooth, shiny threads reflect light, making colours appear lighter and brighter when worked, and matt crewel wools absorb light, making them appear darker and duller.

There is a quite a difference between blending rows of colour into each other (i.e. light to dark) and needlepainting. Needlepainting is the realistic interpretation of colours in a picture or painting—-in other words, we have to copy or scatter the colours as we see them in the picture, and they do not necessarily present themselves in neat little rows! Here are some helpful hints to achieve this:

Subject choice

You can interpret literally any subject in needlepainting, as long as it is not too fussy. When choosing flowers or plants to portray, make sure that the petals and/or leaves have substance, so that you can fill them with long and short stitch. Tiny little petals or berries are not suitable, and will have to be filled with satin stitch. A clear photograph with not too much background is fine as a source, but I prefer to use botanical paintings or prints as the flowers are clearly outlined, with no background details. These can be found as greeting cards, wrapping paper, decoupage prints, books or prints. Detailed watercolour paintings are ideal.

Choosing colours

Look at your source picture or painting and match up your colours carefully. This will sometimes entail the selection of ten or more shades of pink to achieve just the right effect in, say, a pink flower. These shades of colour will be worked alternately or scattered across or down as depicted in the picture you are copying.

Light source

Any realistic picture has a light source, which results in some areas of the motif being in light and some in shadow. This provides dimension, without which the subject would appear flat and lifeless. It is helpful to decide where the light source is coming from, and note where the areas of light and dark will fall. Opposite are some examples of leaves at various angles with the light source shining on them from the top left. Note where the areas of light and shadow fall on each one.

These areas of light and shadow will need to be incorporated into your stitching—the highlights are often a whiter/very pale shade, and the shadows a dark, dull shade, of the colour used. For instance, if you are using shades of pink from light to dark, the highlights could be an off-white or very pale pink and the shadows a dull intensity of the darkest shade of pink.

Adding in detail

Keep it simple, less is more. Do not try to include every little detail of your subject into the stitching, as this will result in a muddled, messy appearance which detracts from the beauty of your shading.

light source

Look at your picture and decide on the values of light to dark of your main colour. Say the picture you are copying is a pink flower with detailed veins and folds in various tones of mauve/rust, do not allow yourself to be distracted by the details. Choose a range of pink values from light to dark and use these as the basis for shading your flower. Next choose a much lighter tone of pinky mauve/rust and a duller tone of pinky mauve/rust to blend in with your main shades of pink. These other tones will create highlights and shadows giving the illusion of the detailed veins and folds. If it is necessary to add in details such as veins, stitch these in afterwards (on top of the main stitching. If the veins are very prominent—for example, the centre vein of a leaf—leave a small gap down the centre and stitch the vein in afterwards in split stitch.

To create the illusion of a vein/fold in a flower, work the lighter values next to the darker values in the appropriate places, to give a three-dimensional effect. To create the illusion of veins you can bring down some of the darker stitches into subsequent rows at intervals and merge these in with the lighter shades. When stitching in dark lines as veins, overlap a few stitches in lighter shades to create a soft, smudged look, thus avoiding rigid lines, as shown in the pansy and Iceland poppy projects.

If the subject has definite details, such as a brown edge on a leaf, work in staggered, small, straight stitches along the edge afterwards but make sure that they blend well into the other leaf colours. A good example of this is the leaves on the rose project. Another example is the brown edges on the leaves of the protea project which are worked in split stitch. Other prominent details such as flower centres can be added in afterwards using the appropriate stitch (i.e. French knots) to add texture for a realistic effect as shown in the Iceland poppy and hibiscus projects.

Scattering colours

Sometimes you will need to scatter colours randomly within a motif, shade across a row, or place a colour to accent highlights or shadows. Don't become confused by the overall mix of colours within your motif, but divide the shape into imaginary rows or slices and copy the colours from your picture into these rows (do not try to use every colour in the picture, remember to choose only the central colours). You can do this by changing values when needed (work on areas of colour), or you can have more than one needle threaded with different values and keep these on top of your work, pinned to the side, so than you can change values when needed. You will notice that in some of the projects I have given two different values for each colour symbol—for example, light pink = 818 and 819. These will be worked alternately across a row, and the next values, that is, the medium pinks, will be blended in with them on the next row. Here is an example of scattering colours across a row, in a petal from the bearded iris project.

Tips for scattering colour

• Look closely at the colours in the picture you are copying.

• Remember you are trying to create an illusion of these colours and will not be able to introduce *every* colour so use the closest central colours. If your painting seems to have 25 shades of pink, for example, reduce them to 10 values.

• Imagine that the shape you are going to stitch is sliced up into rows.

• Take each row individually and decide where you are going to place the colours/shades across the row. (You can pencil in areas of light and dark to assist you.)

• Start stitching with the first colour/shade and then change to the next, working across the row.

- To do this you can work each area of the same colour first or keep several needles threaded in the different colours at the top of your work and use as needed. (If you need to carry your thread across a wide gap when working on an area of colour, use a few tiny running stitches to get there—*do not carry the thread across in one leap.*)

- Start on the next row and do the same bringing, down some of the shades from the first row into the next row if needed. Copy the areas of colour on your picture as closely as possible, concentrating on areas of light, dark and in-between.

- When working values of colour across a row, try not to jump from, say, light pink to dark pink. Work a few stitches of medium pink in between to blend the light and dark pinks together.

- Go back and add in stitches afterwards if necessary. (Be careful not to build up layer upon layer so that the embroidery looks thick and unsightly.) You may need to work some of the shades in a row up into a previous row or down into the next row to get the right placement (see painting with your needle, below).

Painting with your needle

In needlepainting the rows become mixed and encroach into each other to obtain the realism of the picture you are copying. Let go of rigid, row-by-row blending and let the colours from one row flow into another, shading across and down as needed. You will literally feel as though you are painting with your needle, creating brushstrokes with each stitch. Go back afterwards and blend in colours if necessary, merging these stitches into the previous stitches or bleeding between stitches so that they do not look as though they have been added on top. Do not try to create neat little rows of shading, but let some of your stitches go down into the next row space and others split well back into previous rows. As you gain confidence your work will become free and more lifelike.

Add in detail with pencil

It is very helpful to draw in detailed directional lines. I also sketch in outlines of light and dark areas and lightly pencil in sections of shadow. If you do this, use a lighter pencil for adding in details so that they do not become confused with your main outlines. Do not pencil in all the details for the whole flower, rather draw them in section by section as you work.

Layers

Another important aspect of creating dimension is to embroider your picture in layers. Start with the areas that are furthest away (behind) and build up to those in the front. This will lead the eye to the focal points and make the back areas appear to recede slightly.

You can also make some details recede and others come forward through the use of colour. The brighter, lighter colours stand out and the darker colours ebb away—for example, the lighter area on the crease of a petal will make it seem to advance while the darker, shadowed area lying next to this will seem to recede. It is worth taking this into consideration in the overall picture—in other words, use slightly duller colours in the background features and slightly brighter colours in the foreground.

NEEDLEPAINTING EXAMPLE STEP BY STEP

To clarify the needlepainting techniques I have included here the detailed stitching of the large petal from the purple bearded iris project in five steps:

DMC stranded cotton

pale purple	153
light purple	554
dull light purple	3836
medium purple	553
dull medium purple	3835
dark purple	552
darker purple	327
dark lavender	333
dull dark purple	3834
very dark purple	550
very dark blue	823

Draw in the directional guidelines and outline the shape with split stitch. Starting from the centre of the outside of the petal, work long and short stitch from inside the shape over the split stitch outline.

Continue working long and short stitches out towards one side and then the other until the first row is complete, as shown. Note that I have used pale purple and light purple alternating across the left side of the petal, which is the lighter side, and light purple and dull light purple across the right side, which is in shadow. I have used medium purple and dull medium purple to accent the shadowed areas.

STEP 1

STEP 2

Work the second and third row of stitching using staggered long stitches. Some of the stitches split right back into the previous row and some come forward into the space of the third row. Note that I have used the next shades of dull light purple and medium purple across the whole petal, and incorporated more dull medium purple on the right to accent the darker area and a few stitches of dull medium purple on the left side, as this is lighter. I have worked in a few stitches of dark lavender and dull dark purple into the shadowed areas—-these have been brought up from the first row into the second row.

STEP 3

In this next step I have divided the petal into halves and worked on the right-hand (darker side) only. I have worked the next darker shades of purple up to the centre in very dark purple and finally very dark blue. I have scattered dark lavender around the centre and brought some of the very dark purple down the centre line.

STEP 4

In the final step I have worked on the left-hand side of the petal (lighter side), blending it in with the completed right-hand side. Again I have scattered some of the dark lavender around and down towards the centre line. Finally, I have worked the stamen using straight stitches in shades of light yellow, dark yellow and brown with a few stitches in dark lavender. The underneath is worked in darker colours and then I have built up staggered stitches in lighter shades on top to give a furry effect.

Crewel wool

Crewel wool or 2 strands of cotton are recommended for beginners because the yarn is more substantial, therefore easier to split into. Crewel wool is particularly suited to beginners because the hairiness is very forgiving when it comes to blending shades.

crewel wool

Two strands of cotton

Long and short stitch can be worked successfully in 2 strands. This is a good way to practise the stitch, because it is much easier to split back into the stitches which appear more substantial, but will not give the delicate, fine appearance of a single strand as the individual strands do not always lie flat.

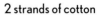
2 strands of cotton

One strand of cotton

When stitching with one strand of cotton, you may find it difficult to split into the previous stitches because the thread is so fine. Work the first row very closely so that you have a good foundation for subsequent rows, and aim to split the thread as often as you can—-if necessary, bleed between stitches, but try to avoid floating stitches (stitches which are not anchored down).

Because the stitches are fine and so close together, you might find it difficult to stagger *each* stitch when blending shades. Don't worry if you find the odd stitch lies in line with the adjacent one—it will still create an illusion of an irregular line when complete.

One strand of cotton is the most suitable yarn to use for needlepainting, as it allows you to introduce fine details and blend colours together.

1 strand of cotton

Silk

Long and short stitch worked in silk thread can be exquisite and should be worked in the same way as one strand of cotton. Most brands of silk are similar in thickness to one strand of cotton, some being slightly thicker or thinner. Find a brand that has a large enough colour range to accommodate your needs.

LONG AND SHORT STITCH FOR DIFFERENT SHAPES

Stitch direction

This is probably the most important aspect of long and short stitch, for if the stitches do not flow smoothly along an imaginary line which corresponds with the grain of a real petal or leaf, the petal or leaf will not look realistic. All stitches are straight and cannot be anything but straight, therefore we need to create an illusion by arranging the stitches to look curved. Each stitch should angle slightly away and cover the end of the previous stitch to form a curve. If each row meshes well with the last you should not be able to see the ends of each row and there will be no hard lines. To blend the colours well you need to ensure that you angle your needle through the stitch and fabric in such a way that you prevent holes from forming, and to ensure that the stitches are anchored down so that no individual stitch shows. Below I give some examples of shapes to be filled:

Filling complex curves

Sometimes the shape that we need to fill has a very complex curve and we need to know how to direct our stitches to follow the shape. When following the curve of a complex shape it may help to shorten your stitches around the curve and increase the number of values of colour to create a smoother transition of colour.

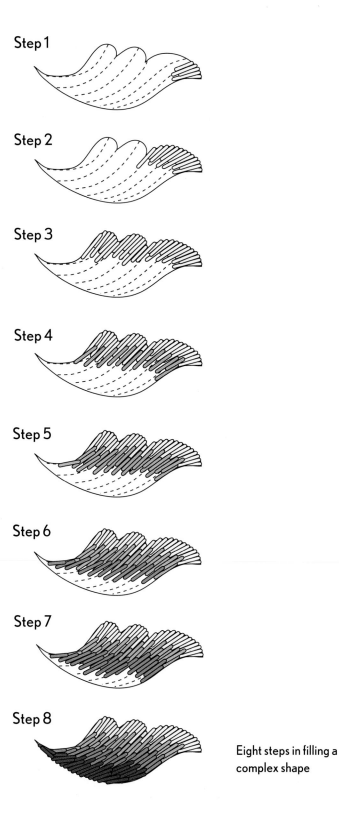

Step 1

Step 2

Step 3

Step 4

Step 5

Step 6

Step 7

Step 8

Eight steps in filling a complex shape

The next two diagrams show how to direct the long and short stitch in other complex shapes.

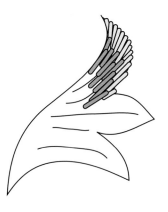

Filling a smooth-edged leaf

Outline the leaf shape and centre vein with split stitch, using the lightest colour thread. Draw in the guidelines with a pencil.

Starting from the outside right edge, and using the lightest colour, work adjoining long and short stitches towards the centre vein. Follow the angle of the guidelines. Continue working the 2nd and 3rd rows in long stitch only, using the next two darkest shades of thread, until you reach the centre vein.

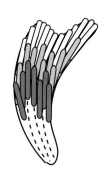

In general, the stitches should radiate out from the point of origin of a shape, such as the centre base of a petal or the centre leaf vein. Wherever possible, start from the outside edge and work in towards this point of origin, or work from a wider area towards a narrow area, because it is easier to reduce stitches than to increase them.

Starting from the outside left edge and using the darkest colour, work adjoining long and short stitches towards the centre vein. Follow the angle of the guidelines. Continue working the 2nd and subsequent rows in long stitch only, using the next lightest shades of thread, until you reach the centre vein.

Having the contrasting light and dark colours meeting at the central vein gives depth to the leaf. Lastly, take one strand of the lightest shade of thread and work the centre vein in split stitch.

A simple way to work small leaves is to shade from light to dark on one side of the centre vein and from dark to light on the other side. If the leaf is very small you can work satin stitch on either side of the centre vein in light and dark shades.

Filling a long leaf

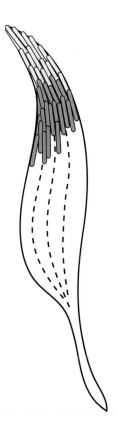

Work the stitches from the tip of the leaf towards the base, shading from light to dark, or work in parallel lines with the lighter colours on one side and darker ones on the other. Some rows of long and short stitch may have to overlap the preceding row to cater for the long narrow shape. It is easier to work this shape of leaf without a split stitch outline to allow long and short stitches to be worked down the sides of the leaf. The veins can be worked in with one strand of split/stem stitch afterwards.

Another very effective way to fill a long leaf shape is to work parallel rows of stem stitch in different shades.

Filling a circular-shaped leaf

With a shape like this it is helpful to divide it into segments and fill in the segments individually, rather than trying to stitch it as a whole. Work the veins in split/stem stitch first—you will see that they all arise from the centre base of the leaf. Then fill each segment with long and short stitch, working from the outside edge in towards the centre base.

Other leaf shapes

In the nine different leaf shapes illustrated here, note the blending of different colours to achieve a realistic effect.

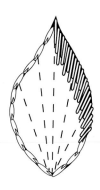

tucked in to the split stitch edge. If the side stitches faced in towards the centre base of the petal they would form a ridge down the centre, giving the illusion of a centre vein. In this case, you could leave it as it is, or go back afterwards and blend in the stitches over and into the ridge to cover it.

Filling petals that overlap

Filling an elongated petal

This diagram illustrates shading the entire outside in a lighter shade, working in towards darker shades in the inside. The side stitches are almost parallel to the side with the bottom ends of the stitches

When filling petals that overlap, the overlap will need to be worked in a lighter shade and the adjoining part of the lower petal in a darker shade to define the edges and make the lower one look shadowed. Work the shadowed section of the underneath petal first, allowing the long and short stitches to run right up to the edge of the petal to be embroidered next (or slightly over it), then work the stem/split stitch outline of the upper petal on top of this stitching.

Filling turnovers on petals or leaves

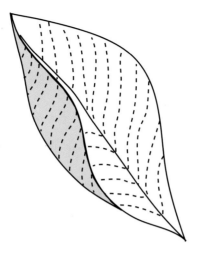

Before you can stitch a turnover on a leaf or petal you need to work out the direction of the stitches on the turnover. An easy way to do this is to draw a rough sketch of the whole petal/leaf on a scrap piece of paper and cut out the shape. Draw in the direction lines on both sides of the paper shape, then fold over the required edge so that the direction lines on the reverse are visible. This method can be used for any shape of leaf or petal. If the turnover is small you may have to change to satin stitch.

Order of working a flower

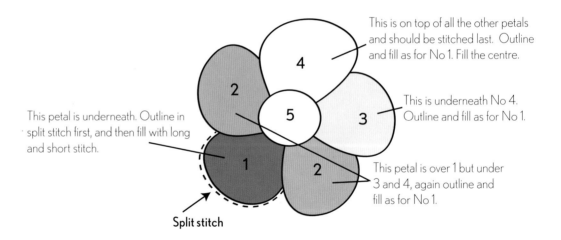

This is on top of all the other petals and should be stitched last. Outline and fill as for No 1. Fill the centre.

This is underneath No 4. Outline and fill as for No 1.

This petal is underneath. Outline in split stitch first, and then fill with long and short stitch.

This petal is over 1 but under 3 and 4, again outline and fill as for No 1.

Split stitch

SATIN STITCH

Satin stitch is used as a filling stitch where a shape is too small to use long and short stitch.

STEP 1 Outline the shape with split stitch.

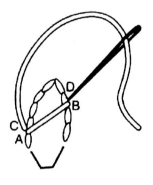

STEP 2 Start from the middle of the shape and work out towards the tip, angling the stitches on the diagonal—-up at A, down at B, up at C, down at D.

STEP 3 Return from the tip to the middle of the shape, slipping the thread under the stitches at the back of the work, and fill the lower half.

Tip for satin stitch

If you are stitching around a curved shape you can work the main satin stitches in the direction of the shape, then go back and fill in the gaps with wedge stitches. The wedge stitches will be tucked inside the main stitches.

PADDING

The projects in this book use only a small amount of padding on areas such as turnovers because I have made more use of highlights and shadows to add dimension. However, I have included directions for padding to give you the option of enhancing certain motifs within your design.

There are two methods. For larger areas you use actual padding material under long and short stitch. For small areas you use two layers of satin stitch.

Long and short stitch over padding

Outline the area to be padded in split stitch. Cut padding material to fit just within each area as shown in the diagram, leaving approximately 1 mm clearance, and slip stitch into place.

You can cut the padded shapes freehand, then trim them to fit, or you can trace the shape onto the padding material with a fine felt-tip pen and cut around it.

When all the padded shapes are in position, embroider over the top with long and short stitch as usual.

Padding with satin stitch

Occasionally an area will be too small to fit in a piece of padding material; in this case you can raise the area with satin stitch. This is very useful for distinguishing the overlap of a leaf or petal.

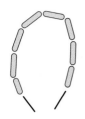

STEP 1 Outline the shape with split stitch.

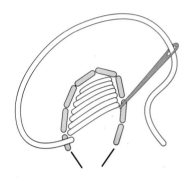

STEP 2 Fill the area with satin stitch on the diagonal, running in the opposite direction to the final layer, taking the needle up and down just inside the split stitch outline.

STEP 3 Work over the shape with a 2nd layer of satin stitch, working on the opposite diagonal, and taking the needle up and down just outside the split stitch outline.

SPLIT STITCH

Split stitch is a variation of a simple backstitch, used to outline shapes and sometimes worked adjacently as a filling stitch for details such as stems. When used as a filling stitch it enables you to shade and change colour within very small spaces, and the results are amazing. This method has become my new preference for filling in smaller details such as stems as it gives more scope for shading in a restricted area.

Commencing with a backstitch, split each preceding stitch with the needle to form the next backstitch.

Tips for split stitch

- When stitching around a curve shorten your stitches.

- To create a more defined or raised outline, use 2 strands for outlining a shape in split stitch.

- It is best to split up through the stitch and not down. If you split up, the back of the work will have a neat running stitch and you will find it is easier to insert your needle very close to the edge of the split stitch outline when working on the front.

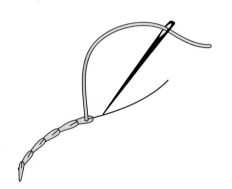

STEM STITCH

Stem stitch is used to work lines such as stems.

The stitches are worked from left to right and overlap each other, without splitting, to form a fine line. When worked adjacently they can be used to fill spaces such as stems and give a fine cord-like effect.

Tips for stem stitch

- When stitching around a curve shorten your stitches.

- When working adjacent rows to fill an area, keep your thread on the outside of the curve as you work.

STRUCTURE OF A FLOWER

It is helpful to understand a bit about the structure of a flower so that you can decide which stitch to use and how each part is positioned. Below is a cross-section of a flower with its parts numbered, and the stitches best suited to interpreting each part listed.

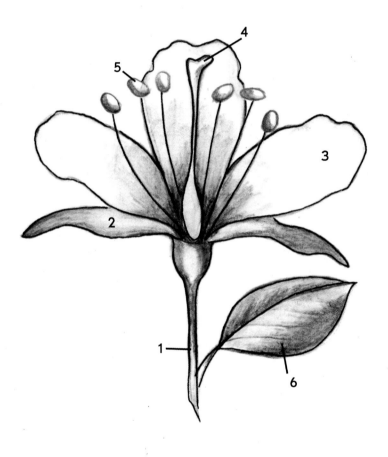

1 Stem Adjacent rows of stem or split stitch.

2 Sepal (small leaves at base of flower) Long and short stitch, or satin stitch if space does not allow for long and short.

3 Petal Long and short stitch, or satin stitch if space does not allow for long and short.

4 Pistil (in centre of flower) Satin stitch, straight stitch or adjacent split stitch.

5 Stamen (from centre of flower with pollen on top) French knots, bullion or straight stitch, depending on the flower.

6 Leaf (from stem) Long and short stitch, or satin stitch if space does not allow for long and short.

STARTER PROJECTS

This section includes four simple folk art flower designs stitched with two strands of thread to get you started and allow you to put long and short stitch into practice. They would make cute little greeting cards, or could be made up as potpourri sachets or linen bags. The designs are stylised and do not need to be interpreted realistically, so feel free to substitute your own colours.

Flower One

MATERIALS

very fine white cotton linen union, 15 cm
    (6 in) square
DMC stranded cottons as in thread key
needle, crewel size 9
small embroidery hoop, approximately
    12cm (4.5 in) diameter
pencil and masking tape

THREAD KEY

DMC stranded cotton

A = light yellow		745
B = yellow		744
C = dark yellow		743
D = light blue		157
E = blue		793
F = dark blue		792
G = light orange		742
H = orange		741
I = dark orange		740
J = very dark orange		946
K = light green		3013
L = green		3012
M = dark green		3011

Tracing outline

Guidelines

Prepare fabric following instructions on page 18.

Transfer the design outline onto your fabric following instructions on page 18.

Mount your fabric into a hoop or frame following instructions on page 20.

Draw in the directional guidelines with a pencil.

Stitch diagram

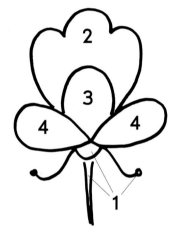

Stitch and colour key

1. K, L, M (stem stitch, satin stitch, French knot, split stitch)
2. A, B, C (split stitch, long and short stitch)
3. D, E, F (split stitch, long and short stitch)
4. G, H, I, J (split stitch, long and short stitch)

All embroidery is worked with 2 strands. Use the colour photo as a guide.

1 Stem, base and tendrils Fill the stem with adjacent rows of stem stitch shading from light to dark green. Fill the base with satin stitch in light green. Fill the tendrils with stem stitch in green and work a French knot at the end.

2 Top petal Outline the top of the petal shape with split stitch. Starting from the top outside edge, working in towards the centre, fill the shape with long and short stitch, shading from light to dark yellow.

3 Centre base petal Outline the top of the petal shape with split stitch. Starting from the top of the petal shape, fill with long and short stitch, shading from light to dark blue towards the centre.

4 Base petals Outline both petals with split stitch. Starting from the outside edge, fill the shapes with long and short stitch, shading from light to dark orange in towards the centre.

Flower Two

MATERIALS

very fine white cotton linen union,
  15 cm (6 in) square
DMC stranded cottons as in thread key
needle, crewel size 9
small embroidery hoop, approximately
  12 cm (4 ½ in) diameter
pencil and masking tape

THREAD KEY

DMC stranded cotton

A = light blue		3839
B = blue		3838
C = dark blue		792
D = very dark blue		791
E = pale rust		3855
F = light rust		3827
G = rust		977
H = dark rust		976
I = very dark rust		975
J = light green		3013
K = green		3012
L = dark green		3011

Tracing outline

Guidelines

PREPARATION

Prepare fabric following instructions on page 18.

Transfer the design outline onto your fabric following instructions on page 18.

Mount your fabric into a hoop or frame following instructions on page 20.

Draw in the directional guidelines with a pencil.

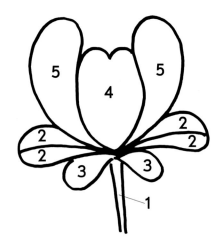

Stitch diagram

Stitch and colour key

1   J, K, L (stem stitch)
2   F, G (split stitch, satin stitch)
3   B, D (split stitch, long and short stitch)
4   A, B, C, D (split stitch, long and short stitch)
5   E, F, G, H, I (split stitch, long and short stitch)

EMBROIDERY

All embroidery is worked with 2 strands. Use the colour photo as a guide.

1 Stem Fill the stem with adjacent rows of stem stitch, shading from light to dark green.

2 Base petals (gold) Outline the petals with split stitch. Fill each side of the petals with diagonal satin stitch using the lighter shade of rust on the top half and the darker shade on the bottom half.

3 Base petals (blue) Outline the petals with split stitch. Fill each petal with long and short, working from the outside edge in towards the centre, shading from light to dark blue.

4 Flower centre Outline the top of the shape with split stitch. Fill with long and short stitch, working from the outside edge in towards the centre, shading from light to dark blue.

5 Petals Outline the petals with split stitch. Fill each petal with long and short stitch, working from the outside edge in towards the centre, shading from light to dark rust.

Flower Three

MATERIALS

very fine white cotton linen union, 15 cm
(6 in) square
DMC stranded cottons as in thread key
needle, crewel size 9
small embroidery hoop, approximately
12 cm (4 ½ in) diameter
pencil and masking tape

THREAD KEY

DMC stranded cotton

A = pale lilac		211
B = light lilac		210
C = lavender		155
D = dark lavender		3746
E = light turquoise		3849
F = turquoise		3848
G = light green		3013
H = green		3012
I = dark green		3011

Tracing outline

Guidelines

Prepare fabric following instructions on page 18.

Transfer the design outline onto your fabric following instructions on page 18.

Mount your fabric into a hoop or frame following instructions on page 20.

Draw in the directional guidelines with a pencil.

Stitch diagram

Stitch and colour key

1   G, H, I (stem stitch)
2   E, F (split stitch, long and short stitch)
3   A, B, C, D (split stitch, long and short stitch)
4   E, F (stem stitch, French knots)

EMBROIDERY

All embroidery is worked with 2 strands. Use the colour photo as a guide.

1 Stem Fill the stem with adjacent rows of stem stitch, shading from light to dark green.

2 Base petals Outline the base of the petals only with split stitch. Fill each petal with long and short stitch, shading from light to dark turquoise.

3 Petals Outline each petal with split stitch. Fill each petal (starting with the lower petals) with long and short stitch, working from the outside edge in towards the centre, shading from light to dark lilac/lavender.

4 Tendrils Fill the tendrils in stem stitch using turquoise and work a French knot at the end of each.

Flower Four

MATERIALS

very fine white cotton linen union, 15 cm
(6 in) square
DMC stranded cottons as in thread key
needle, crewel size 9
small embroidery hoop, approximately
12 cm (4 ½ in) diameter
pencil and masking tape

THREAD KEY

DMC stranded cotton

A = pale mauve		153
B = light mauve		3836
C = mauve		3835
D = dark mauve		3834
E = very dark mauve		154
F = pale gold		746
G = light gold		3047
H = gold		3046
I = dark gold		3045
J = light green		3013
K = green		3012
L = dark green		3011

Tracing outline

Guidelines

PREPARATION

Prepare fabric following instructions on page 18.

Transfer the design outline onto your fabric following instructions on page 18.

Mount your fabric into a hoop or frame following instructions on page 20.

Draw in the directional guidelines with a pencil.

EMBROIDERY

All embroidery is worked with 2 strands. Use the colour photo as a guide.

1 Stem Fill the stem with adjacent rows of stem stitch, shading from light to dark green.

2 Flower centre Outline the shape with split stitch. Work from the tip down towards the base, filling with long and short stitch, shading from light to dark mauve.

3 Outside petals Outline the shapes with split stitch. Fill each petal with long and short stitch, working from the outside edge in towards the centre, shading from light to dark gold.

Stitch diagram

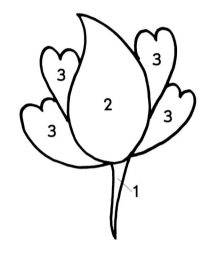

Stitch and colour key

1   J, K, L (stem stitch)
2   A, B, C, D, E (split stitch, long and short stitch)
3   F, G, H, I (split stitch, long and short stitch)

SMALL FLOWER MOTIFS

This section includes three individual, semi-realistic flower motifs, stitched with one strand of thread, which can be used to make up smaller projects. They are an ideal way to familiarise yourself with this style of embroidery before embarking on the larger projects. They would make lovely focal points for a cushion cover or could be framed, as a set or individually.

Red Anemone

MATERIALS

very fine white cotton linen union, 15 cm (6 in) square

DMC stranded cottons as in thread key

needles, crewel sizes 9 and 10

small embroidery hoop, approximately 12 cm (4.5 in) diameter

pencil and masking tape

THREAD KEY

DMC stranded cotton

A = light orange	742
B = orange	740
C = dark orange	608
D = red	666
E = brown	938
F = dark brown	3371
G = light gold	372
H = gold	370
I = light khaki	372
J = khaki	370
K = dark khaki	3011
L = light green	522
M = green	520

Tracing outline

Guidelines

PREPARATION

Prepare fabric following instructions on page 18.

Transfer the design outline onto your fabric following instructions on page 18.

Mount your fabric into a hoop or frame following instructions on page 20.

Draw in the directional guidelines with a pencil.

Stitch diagram

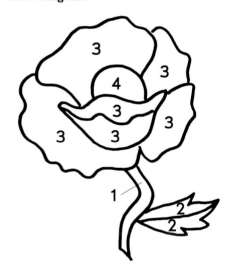

Stitch and colour key

1   I, J, K (stem stitch)
2   L, M (split stitch, satin stitch)
3   A, B, C, D (split stitch, long and short stitch)
4   E, F, G, H (French knots)

EMBROIDERY

All embroidery is worked with 1 or 2 strands as specified. Use the colour photo as a guide.

1 Stem Fill the stem with adjacent rows of stem stitch in 2 strands, shading from dark to light khaki.

2 Leaf Outline the leaf with split stitch in 2 strands. Fill each side of the leaf with satin stitch in 1 strand of either light green or green.

3 Petals Outline each petal with split stitch in 2 strands. Using 1 strand fill each petal (starting with the back petals) with long and short stitch, working from the outside edge in towards the centre and shading from light orange to red.

4 Flower centre Fill the centre with French knots in 2 strands, starting with dark brown, and ending with light gold.

Sunflower

MATERIALS

very fine white cotton linen union, 15 cm
  (6 in) square
DMC stranded cottons as in thread key
needles, crewel sizes 9 and 10
small embroidery hoop, approximately
  12 cm (4 ½ in) diameter
pencil and masking tape

THREAD KEY

DMC stranded cotton

A = pale yellow	3078
B = light yellow	726
C = yellow	728
D = dark yellow	783
E = light khaki	3013
F = khaki	3012
G = dark khaki	3011
H = light green	165
I = green	733
J = dark green	732
K = light brown	435
L = brown	433
M = dark brown	938

Tracing outline

Guidelines

Stitch and colour key

1 E, F, G (stem stitch)
2 H, I, J (split stitch, long
    and short stitch)
3 A, B, C, D (split stitch,
    long and short stitch)
4 K, L, M (French knots)

PREPARATION

Prepare fabric following instructions on page 18.

Transfer the design outline onto your fabric following instructions on page 18.

Mount your fabric into a hoop or frame following instructions on page 20.

Draw in the directional guidelines with a pencil.

EMBROIDERY

All embroidery is worked with 1 or 2 strands as specified. Use the colour photo as a guide.

1 Stem Fill the stem with adjacent rows of stem stitch, using 2 strands and shading from dark to light khaki.

2 Leaf Outline the leaf with split stitch, using 2 strands. Working from the outside in towards the centre vein, fill on either side of the leaf with long and short stitch using 1 strand. Shade from light to dark green, and from dark to light green. Work the centre vein in split stitch using 1 strand light green.

3 Petals Outline each petal in split stitch, using 2 strands. Working from the top edge in towards the centre, fill each petal in long and short stitch, using 1 strand and shading from light to dark yellow. (Start with the back petals and work forwards.)

4 Flower centre Fill the centre with French knots using 2 strands. Shade from dark to light brown.

Purple Bellflower

MATERIALS

very fine white cotton linen union, 15 cm
    (6 in) square
DMC stranded cottons as in thread key
needles, crewel sizes 9 and 10
small embroidery hoop, approximately
    12 cm (4 ½ in) diameter
pencil and masking tape

Tracing outline

THREAD KEY

DMC stranded cotton

A = pale lilac		153
B = light lilac		209
C = lilac		208
D = dark lavender		333
E = pale gold		3822
F = gold		728
G = dark gold		783
H = light khaki		3013
I = khaki		3012
J = dark khaki		3011
K = light green		472
L = green		471

PREPARATION

Prepare fabric following instructions on page 18.

Transfer the design outline onto your fabric following instructions on page 18.

Mount your fabric into a hoop or frame following instructions on page 20.

Draw in the directional guidelines with a pencil.

EMBROIDERY

All embroidery is worked with 1 or 2 strands as specified. Use the colour photo as a guide.

1 Stem Fill stem with adjacent rows of stem stitch, using 2 strands, shading from light to dark gold/khaki.

2 Leaves Outline leaves with 2 strands of split stitch. Pad leaves with loose satin stitches in the opposite direction to stitching. Fill leaves in diagonal satin stitch using 1 strand of light or dark green on either leaf.

3 Petals Outline each petal in 2 strands of split stitch. Working from the outside in towards the centre, fill each petal (starting with the back petal) with long and short stitch, using 1 strand of thread and shading from light to dark lilac/lavender. Fill the base of the flower with long and short stitch, shading from dark to light lavender towards the base.

4 Flower centre Fill the centre with French knots using 2 strands of thread. Shade the knots from dark to light gold.

Guidelines

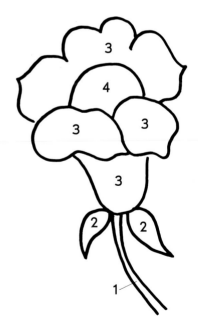

Stitch diagram

Stitch and colour key

1   H, I, J (stem stitch)
2   K, L (split stitch, satin stitch)
3   A, B, C, D (split stitch, long and short stitch)
4   E, F, G (French knots)

FLOWER PROJECTS

This section includes projects stitched with 1 strand of thread, which realistically interpret flower paintings and vary from simple to challenging.

Rose

MATERIALS

very fine white linen union, 20 x 22 cm
  (8 x 9 in)
DMC/Anchor stranded cottons as in thread
  key
needles, crewel sizes 9 and 10
stretcher frame, 16 x 18 cm (6 ½ x 7 in)
pencil and masking tape

THREAD KEY

DMC and Anchor stranded cotton

A = off-white	3865
B = pale pink	819
C = light pink	818
D = medium pink	761
E = dusky pink	152
F = medium dark pink	3326
G = dark pink	3833
H = very dark pink	3328
I = cream	746
J = pale yellow	745
K = yellow	3855
L = pale green	842 (Anchor)
M = light green	858 (Anchor)
N = green	859 (Anchor)
O = light leaf green	3348
P = leaf green	471
Q = dark leaf green	469
R = very dark leaf green	936
S = brown	830

Tracing outline

Guidelines

Stitch diagram

Stitch and colour key

1. O, P, Q, R (split stitch)
2. O, P, Q, R, S (split stitch, long and short stitch, straight stitch)
3. L, M, N (long and short stitch, satin stitch, split)
4. A, B, C, D, E, F, G, H, I, J, K (split stitch, satin stitch, long and short stitch)

PREPARATION

Prepare fabric following instructions on page 18.

Transfer the design outline onto the fabric following instructions on page 18.

Mount the fabric into a frame (for preference) or a hoop following instructions on page 20.

Draw in the directional guidelines with a pencil.

EMBROIDERY

All embroidery is worked with 1 strand unless otherwise specified.

1 Stem Work adjacent rows of split stitch shading from dark to light leaf green, across and down.

2 Main leaves Outline both leaves in split stitch leaving the centre vein free. Fill either side of each leaf with long and short stitch shading from light to dark or dark to light in leaf greens. Make small straight stitches at the outside edge of the leaf in brown.

3 Sepals Outline the sepals in split stitch and fill with long and short stitch shading from light to dark green. Work underside of sepal with satin stitch.

4 Petals and turnovers Start with the back petals and work forward. Outline each petal with split/stem stitch (I used 2 strands of split stitch to define the larger petals). Fill each petal with long and short stitch or satin stitch when space does not allow. Starting from the outside edge in towards the centre, work each petal with shades of pink blending into yellows or deeper pinks. Work the larger turnovers in long and short stitch and the smaller turnovers in satin stitch, shading across the turnover. Use the photo as a guide to the colour placement and shading.

Rosebud

MATERIALS

very fine white linen union, 20 x 22 cm
(8 x 9 in)
DMC/Anchor stranded cottons as in thread key
needles, crewel sizes 9 and 10
stretcher frame, 16 x 18 cm (6 ½ x 7 in)
pencil and masking tape

THREAD KEY

DMC and Anchor stranded cotton

A = pale green	842 (Anchor)	J = light pink	818
B = light green	3348	K = light medium pink	761
C = medium green	471	L = medium pink	3326
D = dark green	3012	M = dark pink	3833
E = very dark green	3011	N = very dark pink	3328
F = light sage green	858 (Anchor)	O = cream	746
G = medium sage green	859 (Anchor)	P = pale yellow	745
H = dark sage green	860 (Anchor)	Q = brown	830
I = pale pink	819		

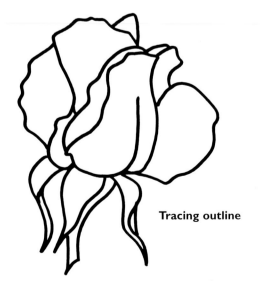

Tracing outline

Guidelines

PREPARATION

Prepare fabric following instructions on page 18.

Transfer the design outline onto the fabric following instructions on page 18.

Mount the fabric into a frame (for preference) or a hoop following instructions on page 20.

Draw in the directional guidelines with a pencil.

EMBROIDERY

All embroidery is worked with 1 strand unless otherwise specified.

1 Stem Work adjacent rows of split stitch, shading from dark to light green, across and down.

2 Sepals Outline sepals in split stitch. Fill each sepal with long and short stitch, shading from dark to light in sage greens. Work a few split stitches in brown at the tips of the sepals.

3 Petals and turnovers Start with the back petals and work forwards. Outline the petals in split stitch and fill with long and short stitch, shading from light to dark pink into yellows. Work in any details or accents afterwards in split stitch. Work the turnovers in long and short stitch or diagonal satin stitch when space does not allow. Use the colour photo as a guide to colour placement and shading.

Stitch diagram

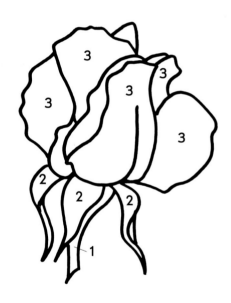

Stitch and colour key

1 A, B, C, D, E (split stitch)
2 F, G, H, Q (split stitch, long and short stitch)
3 I, J, K, L, M, N, O, P (long and short stitch, satin stitch, split stitch)

Cream Pansy

MATERIALS

very fine white linen union, 22 x 24 cm
   (9 x 9 ½ in)

DMC/Anchor stranded cotton as in thread
   key

needles, crewel sizes 9 and 10

stretcher frame, 18 x 20 cm (7 x 8 in)

pencil and masking tape

THREAD KEY

DMC and Anchor stranded cotton

A = cream		746
B = dark cream	386 (Anchor)	
C = pale yellow	300 (Anchor)	
D = yellow	301 (Anchor)	
E = dark yellow		743
F = orange yellow		742
G = dark purple		3746
H = purple		340
I = maroon		3834
J = dark maroon		154
K = pale green	842 (Anchor)	
L = light green	264 (Anchor)	
M = green	265 (Anchor)	
N = dark green	266 (Anchor)	
O = very dark green		469

PREPARATION

Prepare fabric following instructions on
page 18.

Transfer the design outline onto the fabric
following instructions on page 18.

Tracing outline

Guidelines

Draw in the directional guidelines with a pencil.

EMBROIDERY

All embroidery is worked with 1 strand unless otherwise specified.

1 Stem Work adjacent rows of split stitch, shading from dark to light green, across and down.

2 Leaf Outline the leaf in split stitch, leaving the centre vein free. Fill either side of the leaf with long and short stitch, shading from light to dark or dark to light in greens. Work the stem in adjacent rows of stem stitch and the centre vein in stem stitch in light green.

Stitch diagram

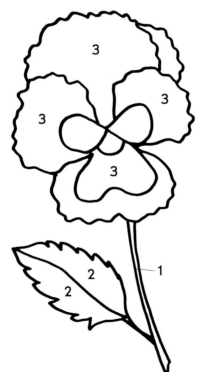

3 Petals Outline the petals in split stitch. Starting with the back petals and working from the outside edge in towards the centre, work long and short stitches in both shades of purple. Change to the cream shades and work from light to dark—encroach right back into the purple and over the split stitch edge at intervals to allow the purple edge to peep through. On the three front petals make long straight stitches in maroon and dark maroon for the centre, staggering them into the yellow section. Work the flower centre details in satin stitch and the orange centre with straight stitches encroaching into the maroon. Go back and work over the petal edges with purple, using small straight stitches to accentuate the frilly edge.

Stitch and colour key
1 L, M, N, O (split stitch)
2 K, L, M, N, O (split stitch, long and short stitch, stem stitch)
3 A, B, C, D, E, F, G, H, I, J (split stitch, long and short stitch, satin stitch, straight stitch)

Mount the fabric into a frame (for preference) or a hoop following instructions on page 20.

Purple Pansy

You will need to study the colour photo for placement of shades, as they encroach into each other and do not necessarily blend from light to dark.

MATERIALS

very fine white linen union, 22 x 24 cm
  (9 x 9 ½ in)
DMC/Anchor stranded cottons as in thread
  key
needles, crewel sizes 9 and 10
stretcher frame, 18 x 20 cm (7 x 8 in)
pencil and masking tape

THREAD KEY

DMC stranded cotton

A = white		blanc
B = pale purple		211
C = light purple		210
D = lavender		155
E = purple		209
F = dark lavender		3746
G = dark purple		333
H = dark blue		792
I = medium purple		208
J = very dark purple		3837
K = light yellow		744
L = yellow		3821
M = pale green		165
N = light green		734
O = green		733
P = dark green		732

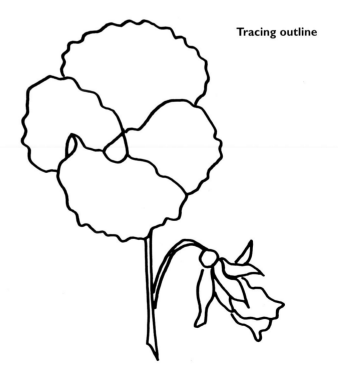

Tracing outline

Guidelines

Stitch diagram

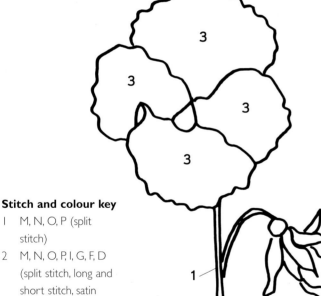

Stitch and colour key

1 M, N, O, P (split stitch)

2 M, N, O, P, I, G, F, D (split stitch, long and short stitch, satin stitch)

3 A, B, C, D, E, F, G, H, I, J, K, L (long and short stitch, satin stitch)

PREPARATION

Prepare fabric following instructions on page 18.

Transfer the design outline onto the fabric following instructions on page 18.

Mount the fabric into a frame (for preference) or a hoop following instructions on page 20.

Draw in the directional guidelines with a pencil.

EMBROIDERY

All embroidery is worked with 1 strand unless otherwise specified.

1 Stems Work adjacent rows of split stitch, shading from dark to light green, across and down.

2 Bud sepals and petals Outline the sepals and bud base in split stitch. Fill each sepal with long and short stitch, shading from light to dark, or dark to light in greens, changing to satin stitch if space does not allow for long and short. Outline bud petals in split stitch and fill each petal with long and short or satin stitch in shades of purple/lavender.

3 Petals Outline the petals in split stitch. Work the back petal first in long and short stitch, shading from light to dark shades of purple/lavender. Alternate colours in each row. Fill the other petals with long and short stitch, using the colour photo as a guide to placement of shades. Work the small turnover on the front petal in satin stitch. Work the centre in satin stitch and encroach the yellow centre into the purples.

Hibiscus

MATERIALS

very fine white linen union, 22 x 24 cm
  (9 x 9 ½ in)
DMC/Anchor stranded cottons as in thread key
needles, crewel sizes 9 and 10
stretcher frame, 18 x 20 cm (7 x 8 in)
pencil and masking tape

THREAD KEY

DMC and Anchor stranded cotton

A = off-white		3865
B = pale purple		153
C = light purple		554
D = medium purple		209
E = dark purple		553
F = plum		3687
G = maroon		150
H = dark cream		3823
I = deep yellow		3855
J = pale leaf green	264 (Anchor)
K = light leaf green	265 (Anchor)
L = medium leaf green	267 (Anchor)
M = dark leaf green	268 (Anchor)
N = pale green	861 (Anchor)
O = light green	842 (Anchor)
P = medium green	213 (Anchor)
Q = dark green	859 (Anchor)
R = very dark green	860 (Anchor)

Tracing outline

Guidelines

Stitch diagram

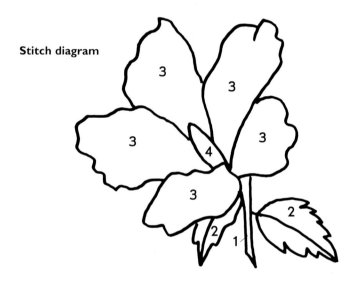

Stitch and colour key

1 O, P, Q, R (split stitch)
2 J, K, L, M, N (split stitch, long and short stitch)
3 A, B, C, D, E, F, G (split stitch, long and short stitch)
4 A, H, I (French knots)

Prepare fabric following instructions on page 18.

Transfer the design outline onto the fabric following instructions on page 18.

Mount the fabric into a frame (for preference) or a hoop following instructions on page 20.

Draw in the directional guidelines with a pencil.

EMBROIDERY

All embroidery is worked with 1 strand unless otherwise specified.

1 Stem Work adjacent rows of split stitch, shading from dark to light green, across and down.

2 Leaves Outline both leaves in split stitch, leaving the centre vein free. Fill either side of each leaf with long and short stitch, shading from light to dark green, or dark to light leaf green.

3 Petals Start with the back petals and work forward. Outline each petal with split/stem stitch (I used 2 strands of split stitch to define the larger petals). Fill each petal with long and short stitch, shading from off-white to dark pink as shown.

4 Flower centre Fill the centre with French knots, shading from off-white to deep yellow.

Iceland Poppy

MATERIALS

very fine white linen union, 22 x 24 cm
   (9 x 9 ½ in)
DMC/Anchor stranded cottons as in thread
   key
needles, crewel sizes 9 and 10
stretcher frame, 18 x 20 cm (7 x 8 in)
pencil and masking tape

THREAD KEY

DMC and Anchor stranded cotton

A = off-white   3865
B = beige   3866
C = pale pink   819
D = light peach pink   3713
E = medium peach pink   761
F = dark peach pink   760
G = dark peach pink   3712
H = pale mauve pink   151
I = light mauve pink   3354
J = medium mauve pink   3733
K = dark mauve pink   223
L = very dark mauve pink   3726
M = light yellow   727
N = medium yellow   3821
O = dark yellow   680
P = pale green   524
Q = light green   858 (Anchor)
R = medium green   859 (Anchor)
S = dark green   860 (Anchor)
T = very dark green   861 (Anchor)
U = pale leaf green   842 (Anchor)

V = light leaf green   843 (Anchor)
W = medium leaf green   844 (Anchor)
X = dark leaf green   845 (Anchor)

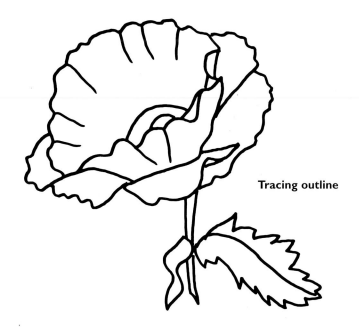

Tracing outline

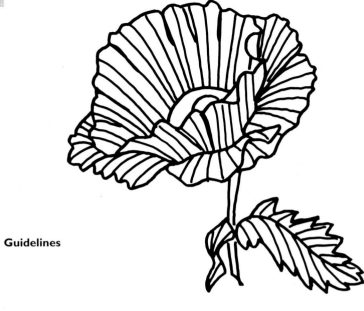

Guidelines

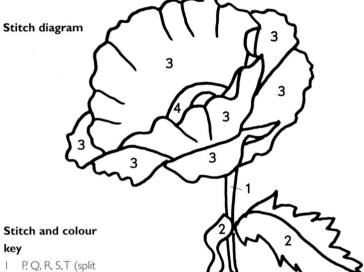

Stitch diagram

Stitch and colour key

1. P, Q, R, S, T (split stitch)
2. U, V, W, X (split stitch, long and short stitch, straight stitch)
3. A, B, C, D, E, F, G, H, I, J, K, L (split stitch, satin stitch, long and short stitch)
4. M, N, O, P, Q, R (French knots)

PREPARATION

Prepare fabric following instructions on page 18.

Transfer the design outline onto the fabric following instructions on page 18.

Mount the fabric into a frame (for preference) or a hoop following instructions on page 20.

Draw in the directional guidelines with a pencil.

EMBROIDERY

All embroidery is worked with 1 strand unless otherwise specified.

1 Stem Work adjacent rows of split stitch, shading from dark to light, across and down.

2 Leaves Outline the large leaf in split stitch, leaving the centre vein free. Fill either side of the leaf with long and short stitch, shading from light to dark green, or dark to light green. Fill the small leaf with long and short, or satin stitch when space does not allow long and short.

3 Petals Start with the back petals and work forward. Outline each petal with split/stem stitch (I used 2-stranded split stitch to define the larger petals). Fill each petal with long and short stitch, or satin stitch when space does not allow long and short. Shade from dark to light peach/mauve pink, using the photo as a guide. Note that the left and centre petal are shaded in mauve pinks and all the others in peach pinks.

4 Flower centre Fill the small centre with French knots, shading in green. Fill the outer centre in French knots shading in yellows.

Arum Lily

MATERIALS

white surface linen, 25 x 36 cm
  (10 x 14 in)
DMC stranded cottons as in thread key
needles, crewel sizes 9 and 10
hoop 21 cm (8 in) diameter, or stretcher
  frame, 20 x 25 cm (8 x 10 in)
pencil and masking tape

THREAD KEY

DMC stranded cotton

A = light golden green	733
B = medium golden green	731
C = dark golden green	730
D = very dark green	936
E = pale green	165
F = light green	3819
G = medium green	581
H = dark green	469
I = white	blanc
J = off-white	3865
K = pale beige	613
L = light beige	612
M = medium beige	611
N = dark beige	610
O = light orange	722
P = dark orange	720

PREPARATION

Prepare fabric following instructions on
page 18.

Transfer the design outline onto the fabric
following instructions on page 18.

Mount the fabric into a hoop or stretcher
frame following instructions on page 20.

Draw in the directional guidelines with a
pencil.

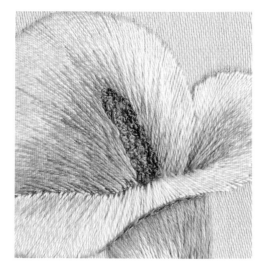

All embroidery is worked with 1 strand unless otherwise specified.

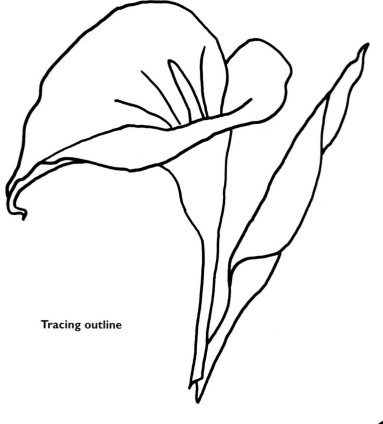

Tracing outline

Guidelines

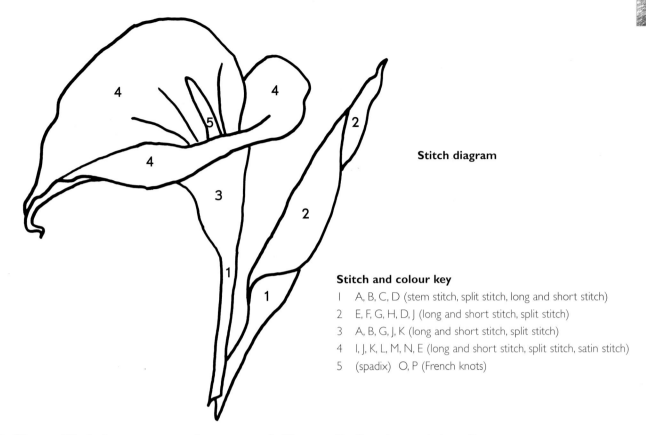

Stitch diagram

Stitch and colour key

1   A, B, C, D (stem stitch, split stitch, long and short stitch)
2   E, F, G, H, D, J (long and short stitch, split stitch)
3   A, B, G, J, K (long and short stitch, split stitch)
4   I, J, K, L, M, N, E (long and short stitch, split stitch, satin stitch)
5   (spadix) O, P (French knots)

1 Stems Work the stems up to the flower base and leaf base in adjacent rows of stem stitch, shading from dark green to light golden green. Work the top of the stems in long and short stitch, shading across.

2 Leaf Outline the leaf in split stitch. Work the background area first in long and short stitch, shading from light to dark green. Work the large turnover in long and short stitch, shading from dark to light green.

3 Base of flower Outline the base in split stitch, joining up with the stem. Fill the base with long and short stitch from the top of the base, blending down into the stem, shading from off-white through to medium green.

4 Flower Outline the petals in split stitch, dividing the sections. Fill the back section first with long and short stitch, shading from white to dark beige towards the centre, and then fill the other sections. Fill the small turnover at the left with satin stitch in off-white. Work a row of split stitch just under the turnover with dark beige to give depth, and blend in a bit of light green in the centre of the flower.

5 Spadix Fill with French knots, shading from dark to light orange.

NB Use the coloured photo as a guide to shading.

Flame Lily

To achieve the flame-like effect so typical of a flame lily it was necessary to blend numerous shades of raspberry into the shades of yellow/beige at the base which, combined, resulted in the red/orange glow. You will need to refer closely to the photograph for placement of colours.

MATERIALS

very fine white linen union, 36 cm (14 in) square

DMC stranded cottons as in thread key

needle, crewel size 10

hoop 23 cm (9 in) diameter, or stretcher frame 23 cm (9 in) square

pencil and masking tape

THREAD KEY

DMC stranded cotton

A = pale green		259
B = light green		165
C = light gold		734
D = gold		733
E = dark gold		732
F = light medium green		3819
G = medium green		166
H = medium dark green		581
I = dark green		580
J = very dark green		937
K = off-white		3865
L = pale grey-brown		3866
M = light grey-brown		644
N = medium grey-brown		642
O = dark grey-brown		640
P = light raspberry		3833
Q = medium raspberry		3832
R = dark raspberry		3831
S = wine red		815
T = dark wine red		814
U = pale yellow		3078
V = light yellow		3822
W = yellow		3821
X = dark yellow		728
Y = tan yellow		729

PREPARATION

Prepare fabric following instructions on page 18.

Transfer the design outline onto the fabric following instructions on page 18.

Mount the fabric into a hoop or stretcher frame following instructions on page 20.

Draw in the directional guidelines with a pencil.

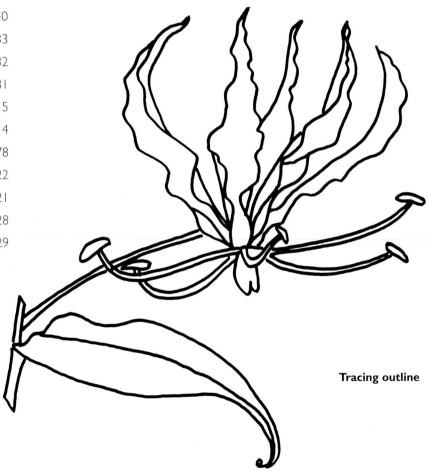

Tracing outline

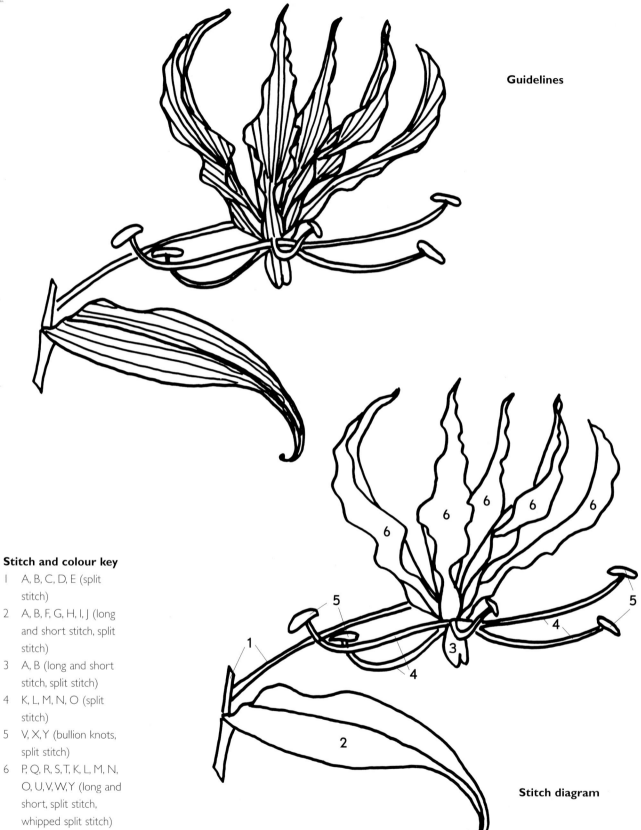

Guidelines

Stitch and colour key

1   A, B, C, D, E (split stitch)

2   A, B, F, G, H, I, J (long and short stitch, split stitch)

3   A, B (long and short stitch, split stitch)

4   K, L, M, N, O (split stitch)

5   V, X, Y (bullion knots, split stitch)

6   P, Q, R, S, T, K, L, M, N, O, U, V, W, Y (long and short, split stitch, whipped split stitch)

Stitch diagram

EMBROIDERY

All embroidery is worked with 1 strand unless otherwise specified.

1 Stems Work the stems in adjacent rows of split stitch, shading from dark gold to pale green across and down.

2 Leaf Outline the leaf in split stitch. Fill either side of the centre vein in long and short stitch, working from the tip of the leaf down towards the base. Shade from light to dark greens across and down, using the photo as a guide.

3 Base of flower Outline the base in split stitch. Fill with long and short stitch, using both shades of green. Work the details in split stitch in grey-brown.

4 Stamens Fill the stamens with adjacent rows of split stitch, using off-white through to dark grey-brown. Use the photo as a guide to shading.

5 Anthers Work a line of split stitch in tan down the centre of the anther. Work a bullion knot on either side of the centre in light yellow and dark yellow, using 1 strand of thread and approximately 10 twists. Anchor the bullions down in the centre with a small stitch.

6 Petals Outline the petals with split stitch in the appropriate colours. Work the back petals first. Starting at the tip, work long and short stitch using shades of raspberry and wine. Work the lower parts of the petals in shades of yellow, and the bases with shades of off-white to grey-brown. Use the photo as a guide. Outline the frilly edges where needed in light yellow split stitch. When the split stitching is complete, take 1 strand of thread and whip the split stitch to define the edges.

NB Use the coloured photo as a guide to shading.

Magnolia

This project will require paying careful attention to the photo and the detail pictures to achieve the subtle blending needed for each individual element of the flower.

MATERIALS

white cotton satin, 43 x 38 cm (17 x 15 in)

DMC stranded cottons as in thread key

needles, crewel sizes 9 and 10

stretcher frame, 30 x 35 cm (12 x 14 in)

pencil and masking tape

THREAD KEY

DMC stranded cotton

A = pale beige		822
B =pale olive green		3013
C =medium olive green		3012
D =medium green		469
E = dark green		936
F = very dark green		934
H = pale brown		3864

Tracing outline

I = light brown	3863	R = medium rust	976
J = medium brown	3862	S = dark rust	301
K = dark brown	3781	T = very dark rust	300
L = light khaki	372	U = white	blanc
M = medium khaki	371	W = off-white	3865
N = light gold	833	X = cream	746
O = medium gold	830	Y = pale tan	739
P = pale rust	3827	Z = light tan	738
Q = light rust	977	ZZ = medium tan	437

Guidelines

PREPARATION

Prepare fabric following instructions on page 18.

Transfer the design outline onto the fabric following instructions on page 18.

Mount the fabric into a stretcher frame following instructions on page 20.

Draw in the directional guidelines with a pencil.

EMBROIDERY

All embroidery is worked with 1 strand unless otherwise specified. You will find the colour photo very helpful as a guide when working this embroidery.

1 Branch Start with the large branch on the right-hand side and outline all the details (scars and other irregularities) in

Stitch diagram

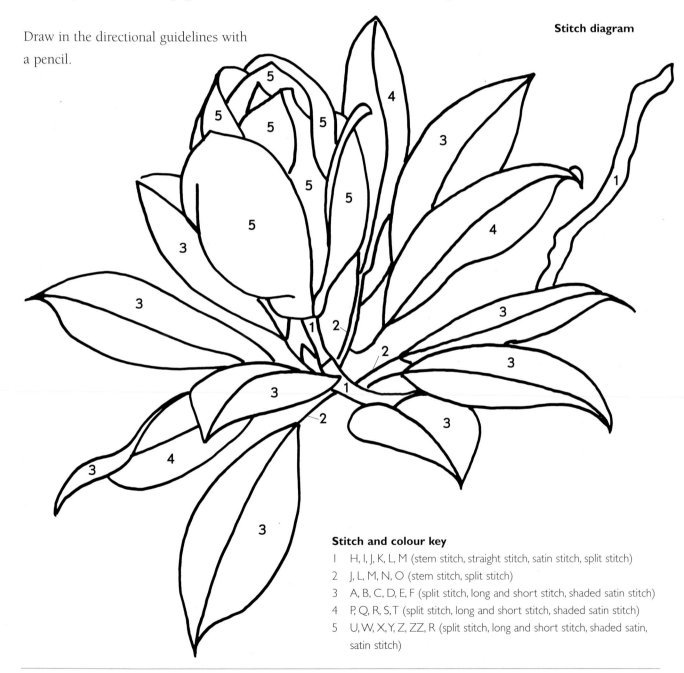

Stitch and colour key

1 H, I, J, K, L, M (stem stitch, straight stitch, satin stitch, split stitch)
2 J, L, M, N, O (stem stitch, split stitch)
3 A, B, C, D, E, F (split stitch, long and short stitch, shaded satin stitch)
4 P, Q, R, S, T (split stitch, long and short stitch, shaded satin stitch)
5 U, W, X, Y, Z, ZZ, R (split stitch, long and short stitch, shaded satin, satin stitch)

dark brown split stitch. Work rows of adjacent stem stitch from the bottom right, shading from dark to light brown. Fill in any details with split stitch or satin stitch.

Work the central part of the branch (among the leaves) with satin stitch, highlighting areas of dark and light. Fill the part of the branch connecting to the flower with rows of adjacent stem stitch in shades of olive green and brown.

2 Leaf stems Work the stems in stem stitch, over or under the branch, and into the base of the leaf.

3 Green leaves Use the min photo as a guide to shading each leaf. Start with the leaves at the back and work forward. Fill each leaf with slanted long and short stitch (or shaded satin stitch if space is insufficient to work long and short) from the outside edge in towards the centre vein, using pale beige through to very dark green. Leave a very small gap for the centre vein. Shade from very light to dark, or vice versa. Work the centre vein with a line of split stitch in the darkest shade of green and another line of split stitch very close to this in light khaki, joining it up with the stems.

4 Rust leaves Use the photo as a guide to shading these three leaves. Start with the back leaves and work forward. Fill each leaf with slanted long and short stitch (or shaded satin stitch if space is too small) from the outside edge in towards the centre vein, using pale to very dark rust. Leave a very small gap for the centre vein. Shade from very light to dark, or vice versa. Work the centre vein with a line of split stitch in the darkest shade of rust and another line of split stitch very close to this in light gold, joining it up with the stems.

5 Flower Use the photo as a guide for shading each petal. Outline all the petals in split stitch in pale tan. Start with the back petals and fill with shaded satin

stitch, or long and short stitch where space allows, using the deeper shades of creams and tans to add depth. Fill the front petals with long and short stitch, shading from white to light tan. Outline some of the details as shown in the photo with medium brown split stitch, and outline the edges of the top petals with 2 strands of split stitch in off-white. Blend in a few straight stitches in pale olive green at the base of the flower.

This project will require detailed attention to the photo and the detail pictures to achieve the subtle blending needed for each individual element of the flower. You will need to mix the colours in each row to achieve the blend of colours.

Purple Bearded Iris

MATERIALS

white surface linen, 40 x 35 cm
    (16 x 14 in)
DMC stranded cotton as in thread key
needle, crewel size 10
stretcher frame, 30 x 25 cm (12 x 10 in)
pencil and masking tape

THREAD KEY

DMC and Anchor stranded cotton

A = pale green		213 (Anchor)
B = light green		369
C = light medium green		858 (Anchor)
D = medium green		859 (Anchor)
E = dark green		3363

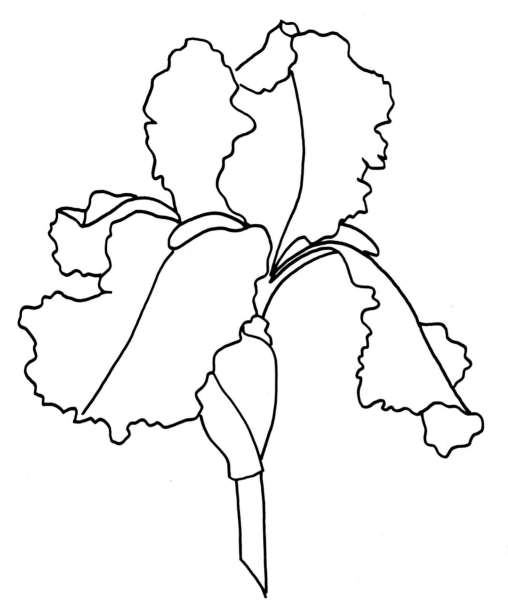

Tracing outline

F = very dark green	3051	Q = pale purple	153
G = lime yellow	445	R = light purple	3836
H = pale lime green	165	S = medium light purple	554
I = light lime green	472	T = medium purple	553
J = medium lime green	471	U = medium dull purple	3835
K = dark lime green	3347	V = dark purple	552
L = light gold	738	W = dark dull purple	327
M = gold	832	X = very dark purple	550
N = brown	167	Y = very dark blue	823
O = light yellow	727	Z = medium lavender	3746
P = dark yellow	3821	ZZ = dark lavender	333

Guidelines

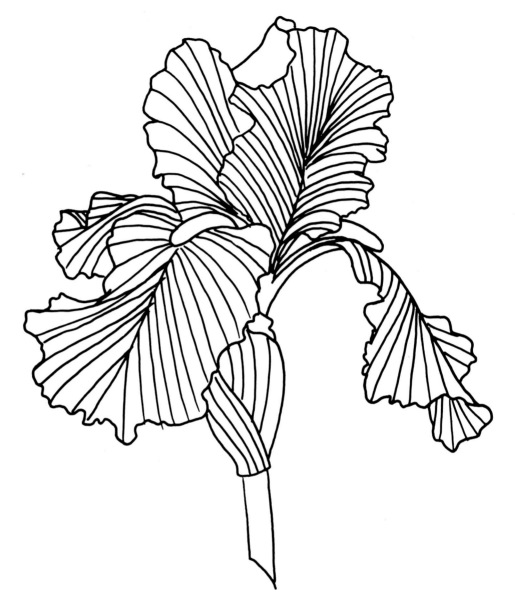

PREPARATION

Prepare fabric following instructions on page 18.

Transfer the design outline onto the fabric following instructions on page 18.

Mount the fabric into a stretcher frame following instructions on page 20.

Draw in the directional guidelines with a pencil.

EMBROIDERY

All embroidery is worked with 1 strand unless otherwise specified. Use the photo as a guide to colour placement.

I Stem Start on the right-hand side with the darkest green and work rows of adjacent split stitch, shading from dark to pale green and then to dark again on the right side.

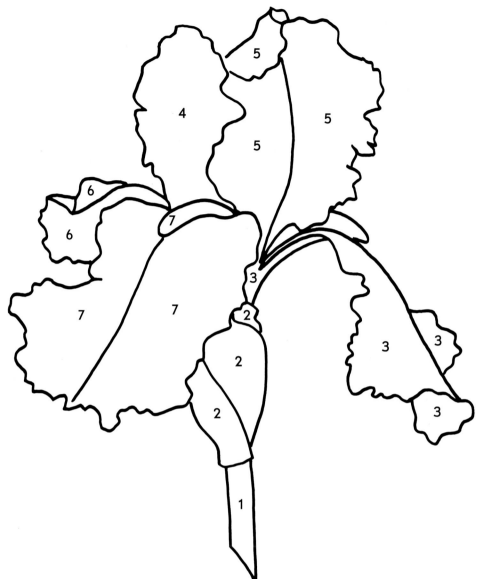

Stitch and colour key

1 A, B, C, D, E, F (split stitch)
2 G, H, I, J, K, L, F (long and short stitch, split stitch, straight stitch)
3 I, J, K, M, O, P, N, Q, R, S, T, U, V, W, X, Y, ZZ (split stitch, long and short stitch, satin stitch, straight stitch)
4 R, S, T U, V, W, X Y (split stitch, long and short stitch)
5 Q, R, S, T U, V, W, X, Y Z, ZZ (split stitch, long and short stitch, straight stitch)
6 R, S T, V, X, Z (split stitch, long and short stitch)
7 Q, R, S, T, U, V, W, X Y, Z, ZZ, M, N, O, P (split stitch, long and short stitch, straight stitch)

2 Base of flower Outline the three sections in split stitch. Start with the large back part of the base and work long and short stitch from the top down to the base, shading from lime yellow to dark lime green. Work in a few stitches in very dark green to accent. Next stitch the front of the base, as before shading from pale lime green through to dark lime green. Work the small top section with straight stitches in light gold and brown.

3 Petal one (right-hand fall) Outline the petal in split stitch. Starting at the base of the petal, work long and short stitch in lime greens. Next work the underneath of the petal (adjacent to the stem) in long and short stitch, from light yellow through to gold. Start stitching the main section of the top surface of the petal from the lower edge up towards the stem base, shading from pale purple through to very dark purple and very dark blue with a few stitches in dark lavender

to accent. Note the underneath of the petal is in dark shades of purple. Next fill the stamen with light yellow, dark yellow and brown straight stitches. Work the light colours first and build up layers to the darker colours to give it a furry effect.

4 Petal two (left-hand standard)

Outline the petal in split stitch. Work long and short stitch from the outside in towards the centre of the flower, shading from light purple to very dark purple and then into very dark blue.

5 Petal three (right-hand standard)

Outline the petal in split stitch. Work the petal in two sections, noting that the left side is darker than the right. Work long and short stitch from the outside edge in towards the centre base, shading from pale purple through to very dark purple and dark blue. Add a few stitches in dark lavender to accent and a few stitches in medium lavender at the base. Next work the turnover in long and short stitch in the lighter shades of purple. Work a few straight stitches in pale and light purple down the centre and finally work a line of split stitch in pale purple to accent the centre vein.

6 Petal four (left-hand fall)

Outline the petal in split stitch. Work this small petal in long and short stitch, or satin stitch when space does not allow long and short, shading from light purple through to very dark purple.

7 Petal five (front fall)

Outline the petal in split stitch. Work long and short stitch from the outside edge in towards the centre, shading from pale purple to very dark purple and dark blue. Add stitches in medium and dark lavender to accent. After the first rows divide the petal into two sections, right and left, noting that the right side is darker than the left. Continue filling each side with long and short until complete. Work a few straight stitches down the centre vein in very dark purple. Finally, fill the stamen with straight stitches, starting with light yellow, dark yellow, brown and a few stitches of dark lavender. Build up layers to give it a furry effect. (See the needlepainting example on page 42 for more detailed stitching instructions for this petal.)

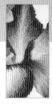

Rust Red Bearded Iris

This project requires some skill. You need to mix the colours in each row to achieve the effect that you need; in other words, the shading has to be worked both across and down. I suggest you pay close attention to the detail in the photo for each individual element of the flower.

Tracing outline

MATERIALS

white surface linen, 43 x 38 cm
(17 x 15 in)
DMC stranded cotton as in thread key

needles, crewel sizes 9 and 10
stretcher frame, 30 x 35 cm (12 x 14 in)
pencil and masking tape

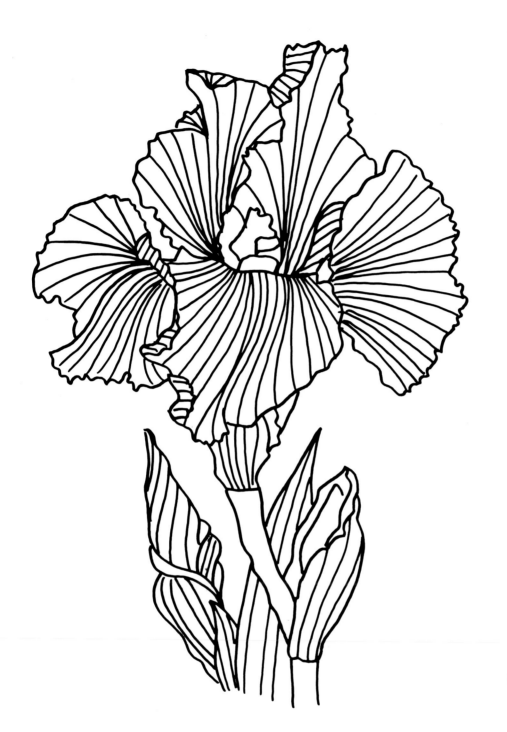

Guidelines

DMC stranded cotton

A = pale green	772	F = pale gold	3047
B = light green	3348	G = light khaki green	3013
C = medium green	3347	H = medium khaki green	3053
D = dark green	3346	I = dark khaki green	3052
E = very dark green	520	J = very dark khaki green	3051
		K = light gold	3046
		L = medium gold	3045

Stitch diagram

Stitch and colour key

1   F, K, M, N, H, I (split stitch, long and short stitch, satin stitch)
2   F, G, H, I, J (split stitch, long and short stitch)
3   A, B, C, D, E (stem stitch)
4   A, B, C, D, F, G (split stitch, long and short stitch, satin stitch)
5   F, K, L, M B, C, D, N (split stitch, long and short stitch, satin stitch)
6   N, M, S, T, W, F, G (split stitch, satin stitch, shaded satin stitch, French knots)
7   P, W, X, Y, Z, ZZ (split stitch, long and short stitch, satin stitch)
8   P, Q, W, X, Y, Z, ZZ, H, I (split stitch, long and short stitch)
9   O, P, Q, R, S, T (split stitch, long and short stitch)
10 O, P, Q, R, S, T, U (split stitch, long and short stitch, satin stitch)
11 O, P, Q, R, S, T, U, Y, ZZ (split stitch, long and short stitch, satin stitch)

M = dark gold	167	T = dark rust	301
N = brown	801	U = very dark rust	300
O = light cream	746	W = pale terracotta	758
P = cream	3823	X = light terracotta	3778
Q = pale rust	3856	Y = medium terracotta	3830
R = light rust	402	Z = dark terracotta	3777
S = medium rust	3776	ZZ = very dark terracotta	3857

PREPARATION

Prepare fabric following instructions on page 18.

Transfer the design outline onto the fabric following instructions on page 18.

Mount the fabric into a stretcher frame following instructions on page 20.

Draw in the directional guidelines with a pencil.

EMBROIDERY

All embroidery is worked with 1 strand unless otherwise specified.

1 Bud on left Start from the right side and work across and down to the centre in long and short stitch, shading from brown to pale gold. Add a few highlights afterwards. Work the base in long and short stitch using golds and browns through to khaki greens from top to bottom, and work the overlap in satin stitch using pale gold.

2 Back leaf Start from the tip and work down in long and short stitch shading from pale gold through to very dark khaki green.

3 Main stem Work adjacent rows of stem stitch, shading from dark to light green.

4 Base of flower Fill with long and short stitch, using pale to dark green from top left down to base. Fill back area with shaded satin stitch in dark greens. Work the turnover with satin stitch in shades of gold. Work base where it meets stem with a row of split stitch in pale gold.

5 Bud on right Work the bud stem in long and short stitch, shading from light to dark green across the stem. Fill the bud centre with long and short stitch in shades of gold to brown and outline with the darkest shade. Fill the outer part of the bud with long and short stitch from the top down to the base, shading from brown to green and pale gold at base. Fill the turnover in satin stitch in pale gold and work a line of brown split stitch just under the edge of the turnover.

6 Flower centre Outline all the compartments of this complex area with split stitch. Fill the two upper sections with shaded satin stitch, using the photo as a guide to colour placement. Fill the lowest section with shaded French knots in pale gold, light khaki and dark gold. You need to create an illusion in this part of the flower, because it is impossible to reproduce the exact details.

7, 8, 9, 10, 11:

7 Petal one (right-hand standard)

8 Petal two (right-hand fall)

9 Petal three (left-hand fall)

10 Petal four (left-hand standard)

11 Petal five (centre front fall)

Outline each petal and all turnovers in split stitch. Fill each petal in long and short stitch, working from the outside edge of each in towards the centre, and shading from dark to light. You will need to alternate shades in a row, or leave gaps and fill in with darker or lighter shades across the row. Work the turnovers in satin stitch or shaded satin stitch, and blend in any details, highlights or darker areas afterwards in straight satin stitch.

NB Use the coloured photo as a guide to shading.

Protea

This project is not as difficult as it may seem at first glance, although there is a lot of stitching in it. Note that the light comes from the top left, so everything on the top left is light and everything on the bottom right is in shadow. The petals change from pink to peachy shades as you work down the flower.

MATERIALS

very fine white linen union, 35 x 30 cm (14 x 12 in)

DMC and Anchor stranded cottons as in thread key

needle, crewel size 10

stretcher frame, 28 x 23 cm (11 x 9 in)

pencil and masking tape

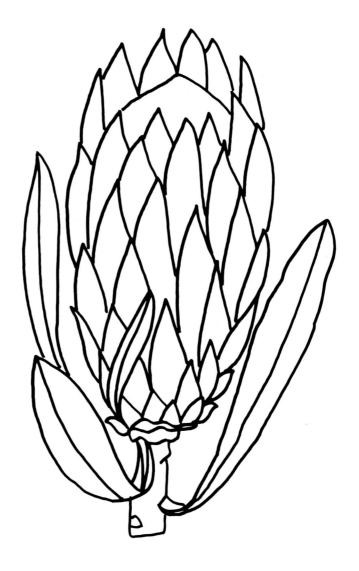

Tracing outline

W = dark rust	920	
X = dark brown	433	
Y = grey	451	
Z = dark grey	645	
TT = white	blanc	
UU = pale green	264 (Anchor)	
VV = light green	471	
WW = medium green	266 (Anchor)	
XX = medium dark green	267 (Anchor)	
YY = dark green	268 (Anchor)	
ZZ = very dark green	3362	

PREPARATION

Prepare fabric following instructions on page 18.

Transfer the design outline onto the fabric following instructions on page 18.

Mount the fabric into a stretcher frame following instructions on page 20.

Draw in the directional guidelines with a pencil.

Stitch diagram

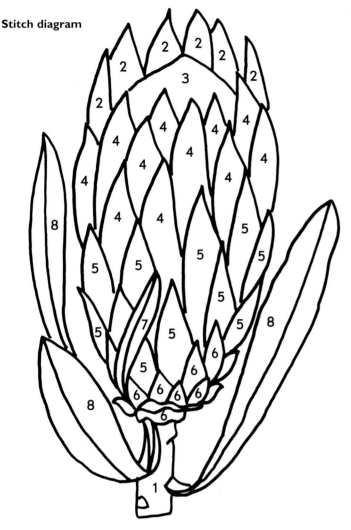

All embroidery is worked with 1 strand unless otherwise specified.

1 Main stem Fill the main stem with adjacent rows of split stitch, using pale ecru through to very dark brown, shading the areas as shown in the photograph. Fill in the notches with dark brown straight stitches.

2 Petals at upper back Outline all the petals at upper back, and the pink and peach petals, with split stitch, using medium pink. Fill these petals with long and short stitch, shading from the top down, in dark to light pink. Remember to use darker shades on the right side of the petals.

3 Flower centre Start at the base of the flower centre and work staggered straight stitches in grey; continue working layers of straight stitches using the darker

Stitch and colour key

1 A, B, C, D, E, F (split stitch, straight stitch)
2 H, I, J, K, L (long and short stitch, split stitch)
3 Y, K, J, H, TT (straight stitch)
4 G, H, I, J, K, L, M, N, O, P, Z, TT (split stitch, long and short stitch, straight stitch)
5 R, S, T, U, V, W, X, M, N, O, P, Q, (split stitch, long and short stitch)
6 N, O, P, Q, W, X, F, TT (split stitch, long and short stitch)
7 UU, VV, WW, XX, YY, N, W, F (split stitch, shaded satin stitch, whipped split stitch)
8 UU, VV, WW, XX, YY, ZZ, W, X F, N, O (split stitch, long and short stitch, whipped split stitch)

shades of pink first and finishing with the white on top. The stitches should gather together at a peak at the top of the flower centre. Note that the centre is lighter on the left and darker on the right.

4 Pink petals Start with the upper petals, working forward and down. Fill each petal with shades of pink into green as they progress down the flower. Outline some areas of the petals with dark grey on the right-hand side (see photograph) to give depth. Make small straight stitches along the tips of the petals in white to give a furry look.

5 Peach petals Fill these petals with long and short stitch, starting with shades of peach, blending into shades of green, as they appear in the photo. Outline the tips and some of the sides of the petals with dark rust to accent them.

6 Small base petals Fill the base petals in shades of green, shading from light to dark. Outline the petals in split stitch, using shades of brown and rust to accent them. Work the tiny petals at the very base in straight stitch in shades of brown and rust. Work a few small stitches in white to accent them.

7 Small leaf on flower Outline the leaf in split stitch. Fill on either side of the centre vein in shaded satin stitch, using lighter colours on the left and darker colours on the right. Outline the right side

of the petal and centre vein with split stitch using the light lime green. Whip the split stitch on the right to accent it and add a few stitches of rust and dark brown at the tip.

8 Large leaves Start with the leaf at upper left. Outline each leaf with split stitch and fill on either side of the centre vein with long and short stitch, shading from light to dark green. Use lighter shades on the left side and darker shades on the right. Fill the centre vein with split stitch in light lime green. Outline in places (see photograph) in whipped split stitch in both shades of lime green (start with light and change to the darker shade). The tips should be worked in shades of brown and rust.

NB Use the coloured photo as a guide to shading.

Pink Sweet Peas

This project requires considerable attention to detail. You need to mix the colours in each row to achieve the effect that you need; in other words, the shading has to be worked both across and down to achieve the depth and light needed to portray the delicate feel of the petals.

MATERIALS

off-white (oyster) linen twill, 35 x 30 cm
    (14 x 12 in)
DMC stranded cottons as in thread key

needles, crewel sizes 9 and 10
stretcher frame, 30 x 25 cm (12 x 10 in)
pencil and masking tape

Tracing outline

THREAD KEY

DMC stranded cotton

A = pale green	369	H = pale brown	644
B = light green	772	I = light brown	642
C = medium light green	3348	J = medium brown	640
D = medium green	3364	K = dark brown	3787
E = dark green	3363	L = pale pink	819 + 818
F = very dark green	3362	M = light pink	151 + 3354
G = very pale brown	822	N = medium pink	3688 + 316
		O = dark pink	3687 + 3726
		P = very dark pink	315

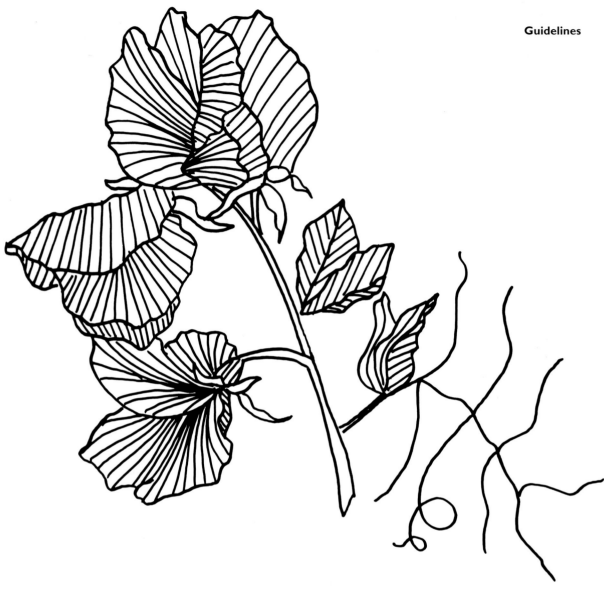

PREPARATION

Prepare fabric following instructions on page 18.

Transfer the design outline onto the fabric following instructions on page 18.

Mount the fabric into a stretcher frame following instructions on page 20.

Draw in the directional guidelines with a pencil.

EMBROIDERY

All embroidery is worked with 1 strand unless otherwise specified.

1 Main stem Start on the left side of the stem and work adjacent rows of stem stitch, shading from darkest green to lightest green.

2 Small brown stems Fill the stems with split stitch, shading from dark brown

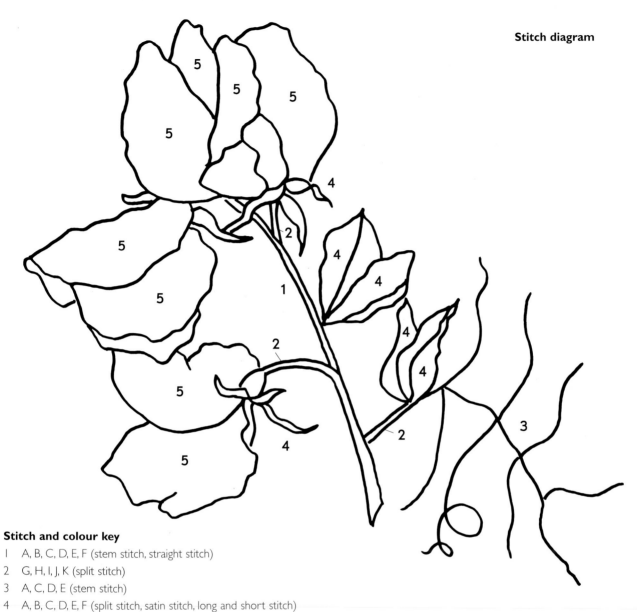

Stitch and colour key

1 A, B, C, D, E, F (stem stitch, straight stitch)
2 G, H, I, J, K (split stitch)
3 A, C, D, E (stem stitch)
4 A, B, C, D, E, F (split stitch, satin stitch, long and short stitch)
5 L, M, N, O, P (split stitch, long and short stitch)

to very pale brown. Use the photo as a guide to shading.

3 Tendrils Work the tendrils in stem stitch, changing to different shades of green. Use the photo as a guide.

4 Leaves and sepals Outline each leaf and sepal in split stitch, using a similar shade of green for each. Fill the sepals (at the bases of the flowers) in satin stitch, or long and short where space allows. Fill the leaves in long and short stitch, using the directional lines as a guide, shading from pale to very dark green. Use the

photo as a guide to colour placement and shading.

5 Petals Outline each petal in split stitch, using a similar shade of pink throughout. Starting with the back petals and working forward, fill each petal with long and short stitch, working from the outside edge in towards the centre and shading from pale to very dark pink,

being guided by the guidelines diagram. I have grouped some of the colours together on the colour key—for example, L, pale pink, 819 + 818—where these need to be used alternately across a row. Use the photo as a guide to the shading.

NB Use the coloured photo as a guide to shading.

Field Poppies

This project requires some skill. You need to mix the colours in each row to achieve the effect that you need; in other words, the shading has to be worked both across and down. I have used a combination of wool and cotton here to show how wool can be used.

off-white (oyster) linen twill, 50 x 40 cm
(20 x 16 in)
DMC stranded cottons as in thread key
Appleton's crewel wool as in thread key
needles, crewel sizes 9, 10 and 4
stretcher frame, 45 x 35 cm (18 x 14 in)
pencil and masking tape

THREAD KEY

DMC stranded cotton and Appleton's crewel wool

A = cream		746
B = pale gold		3047
C = light khaki green		3013
D = medium khaki green		3012
E = medium grey		640
F = pale soft green		524
G = khaki machine embroidery thread		
H = pale grey green		351
I = light grey green		352
J = light Jacobean green	292 (Appleton)	
K = medium Jacobean green	293 (Appleton)	
L = dark Jacobean green	294 (Appleton)	
M = pale drab green	331 (Appleton)	
N = light drab green	332 (Appleton)	
O = medium olive green	343 (Appleton)	
P = dark olive green	344 (Appleton)	
Q = very pale mauve	883 (Appleton)	
R = pale rose pink	141 (Appleton)	
S = light rose pink	142 (Appleton)	
T = light mauve	711 (Appleton)	
W = medium rose pink	144 (Appleton)	
X = dark rose pink	756 (Appleton)	
Y = light bright rose pink	943 (Appleton)	
Z = medium bright rose pink	944 (Appleton)	

WW = medium dark bright rose pink	945 (Appleton)	
XX = dark bright rose pink	946 (Appleton)	
YY= very dark bright rose pink	947 (Appleton)	
ZZ= darkest bright rose pink	948 (Appleton)	
YZ = dark dull mauve	935 (Appleton)	

PREPARATION

Prepare fabric following instructions on page 18.

Transfer the design outline onto the fabric following instructions on page 18.

Mount the fabric into a stretcher frame following instructions on page 20.

Draw in the directional guidelines with a pencil.

EMBROIDERY

All embroidery is worked with 1 strand unless otherwise specified.

1 Main stem at back Start from the top left side and using the medium grey work stem stitch, changing to the next lightest shade of medium khaki green about three-quarters down the stem. Continue working adjacent lines of stem stitch, shading across and down from khaki to pale gold and cream to achieve the effect. Using one strand of khaki machine embroidery thread, work straight stitches randomly to add the spikes.

Tracing outline

Guidelines

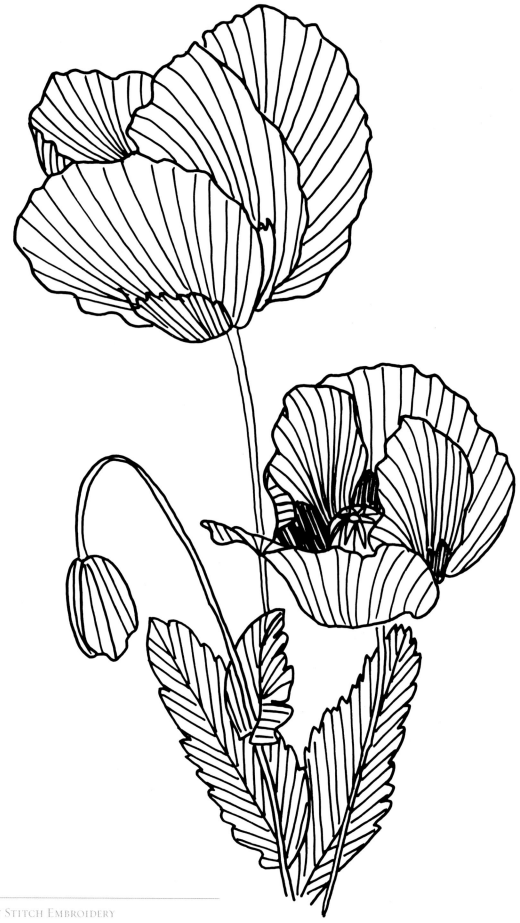

2 Large leaves Outline each leaf in split stitch, using light Jacobean green and leaving a gap for the centre vein. Fill each leaf in long and short stitch, using shades of grey and Jacobean green, shading from the outside edge in towards the centre vein. Work the centre vein in stem stitch using pale green.

3 Small leaf Outline the leaf in split stitch using light drab green, leaving a gap for the centre vein. Fill each side of the vein in long and short stitch, using pale green through to dark drab and olive green. Work the centre vein in split stitch using dark olive green.

4 Short stems at front Work adjacent rows of stem stitch, shading from dark to light, across and down, using medium grey, khaki, pale gold and cream. Using 1 strand of khaki machine embroidery thread, work straight stitches randomly to add the spikes.

5 Bud Fill back area first in dark Jacobean green. Fill front with long and short stitch, working from base to top, using light and medium Jacobean green. Blend in a few long and short stitches at the top in a rose pink shade.

6 Small flower (NB Use the photo as a guide to shading—some of the shades are used alternately across a row.) Start with the large back petal and outline with split stitch. Fill with long and short stitch, working from the outside edge in towards the base, alternating shades of light mauve and medium rose in the first row. Next outline the right petal in stem stitch, then fill as before, shading from pale rose down to the darkest colour. Work the base of the petal in dark dull mauve. Next work the left petal as before, leaving the turnover until last. Fill the turnover in shaded satin stitch. Finally, work the front petal. Outline in stem stitch and fill in long and short stitch, shading across and down to achieve the effect. Make sure that the underside of the turnover is darker. Complete by working the turnover in satin stitch in the lightest shade of pink

7 Flower centre Fill each compartment with satin stitch in medium grey. Fill the centre with satin stitch in the pale soft green. Using 2 strands of the pale gold, work straight stitches from the centre towards the base, creating a slight triangle so that the dark background shows through. Using 1 strand of the pale green, work straight random stitches to create the furry effect around the edge.

8 Large flower (NB Use the photo as a guide to placing shades from very pale mauve/pink through to dark dull mauve at the base of the flower. Each petal uses different shades and some are worked alternately across a row.) Outline the back petals in split stitch using the appropriate shade. Outline the front petals in stem stitch using the appropriate shade. Fill the small back petal first in long and short stitch, shading from the outside edge in

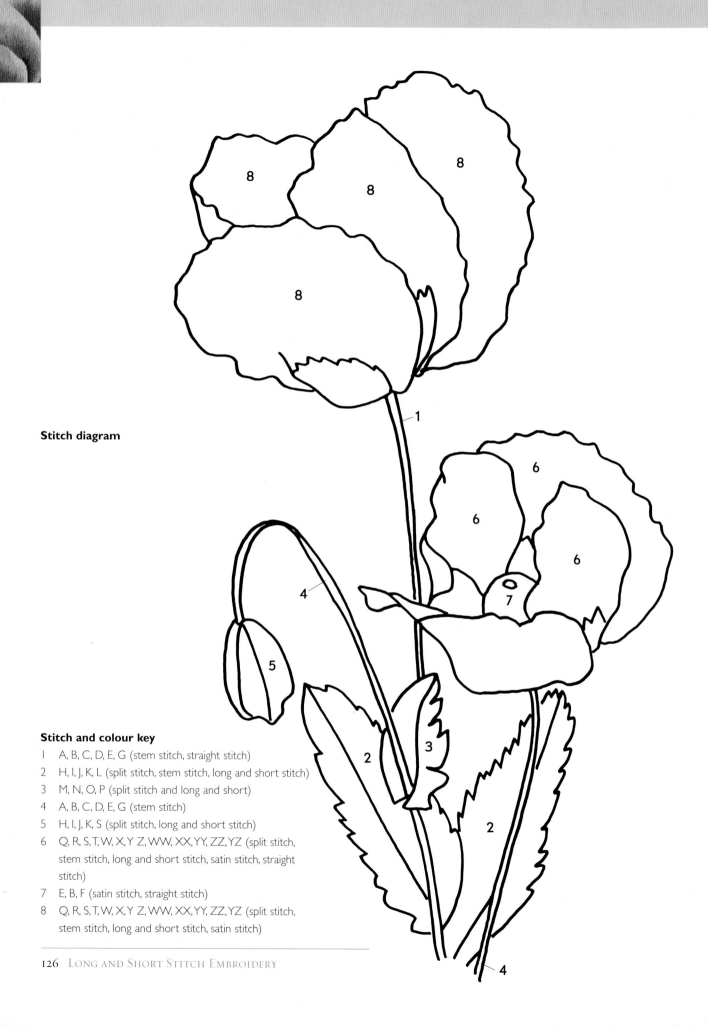

Stitch diagram

Stitch and colour key

1 A, B, C, D, E, G (stem stitch, straight stitch)

2 H, I, J, K, L (split stitch, stem stitch, long and short stitch)

3 M, N, O, P (split stitch and long and short)

4 A, B, C, D, E, G (stem stitch)

5 H, I, J, K, S (split stitch, long and short stitch)

6 Q, R, S, T, W, X, Y Z, WW, XX, YY, ZZ, YZ (split stitch, stem stitch, long and short stitch, satin stitch, straight stitch)

7 E, B, F (satin stitch, straight stitch)

8 Q, R, S, T, W, X, Y Z, WW, XX, YY, ZZ, YZ (split stitch, stem stitch, long and short stitch, satin stitch)

towards the centre. Fill the turnover in pale shades. Work the large back petal next in long and short stitch, shading from the outside edge in towards the centre, alternating shades of colour across and down where necessary. Next fill the centre petal as before. Finally work the front petal as before.

NB Use the coloured photo as a guide to shading.

RECOMMENDED READING

These books all reference long and short stitch embroidery.

Shelagh Amor, *Crewel Embroidery*, Sally Milner Publishing, Bowral, Australia, 2002

Carol Andrews, *Embroideries from an English Garden*, Ruth Bean Publishers, London, 1997

Josiane Bertin-Guest, *Chinese Embroidery Traditional Techniques*, kp books, 2003

A–Z of Thread Painting, Country Bumpkin Publications, Adelaide, 2005,

Trish Burr, *Redouté's Finest Flowers in Embroidery*, Sally Milner Publishing, Bowral, Australia, 2002

Audrey Francini, *Crewel Embroidery with Texture and Thread Variations*, Van Nostrand Reinhold, New York, 1982

Sue Hawkins, *Crewel Embroidery*, David & Charles, Devon, UK, 2001

Jane Rainbow, *Beginner's Guide to Crewel Embroidery*, Search Press, 1999

Sally Saunders, *Royal School of Needlework Embroidery Techniques*, Batsford, London, 1998

Young Yang Chung, *Painting with a Needle*, Harry N Abrams, 2003

SUPPLIERS

Jenny June Fancywork USA (online ordering/mail order service available)
47 VT Route 66, PO Box 367, Randolph, Vermont 05060, USA
Toll-free: 1-800-715-3558
Tel: 802-728-5392
Website: www.jennyjune.com

Mace & Nairn UK (online ordering/mail order service available)
PO Box 5626, Northampton, United Kingdom NN7 2BF
Tel: (44) 1604 864 869
Email: enquiries@maceandnairn.com
Website: www.maceandnairn.com

Crafters Inn South Africa (mail order service available)
9 Morkels Arcade, Main Street, Box 1539, Somerset West, Cape Town, South Africa
Tel: 021 851 5299 Fax: 021 852 4158

Country Bumpkin Australia (online ordering/mail order service available)
315 Unley Road, Malvern, South Australia 5061
Tel: (08) 8372 7600 (within Australia) or +61 8 8372 7600 (outside Australia)
Fax: (08) 8372 7601 (within Australia) or + 61 8 8372 7601
Email: mailorder@countrybumpkin.com.au
Website: www.countrybumpkin.com.au.